THE RETAIL
REVIVAL

THE **RETAIL REVIVAL**

REIMAGINING BUSINESS FOR THE NEW AGE OF CONSUMERISM

DOUG STEPHENS
President, Retail Prophet Consulting

John Wiley & Sons Canada, Ltd.

Library and Archives Canada Cataloguing in Publication

Stephens, Doug
      The retail revival : reimagining business in the new age of consumerism / Doug Stephens.

Includes index.
Issued also in electronic format.
ISBN 978-1-118-48967-3

      1. Consumer behavior. 2. Consumption (Economics).
3. Retail trade. I. Title.

HF5415.32.S74 2013   658.8'342   C2013-900341-X
ISBN 978-1-118-48979-6 (ebk); 978-1-118-48978-9 (ebk); 978-1-118-48980-2 (ebk)

Production Credits
Managing Editor: Alison Maclean
Executive Editor: Don Loney
Production Editor: Pauline Ricablanca
Cover Design: Adrian So
Cover Photography: © Adriana Berned/iStockphoto; © pictafolio/iStockphoto
Composition: Thomson Digital
Printer: Friesens Corporation

Printed in Canada

1 2 3 4 5 FC 17 16 15 14 13

FOR MEREDITH, CONNOR AND REILLY

CONTENTS

ACKNOWLEDGMENTS

THE FOLLOWING PEOPLE were invaluable in supporting the creation of this work:

Andy Bruce for the coffee and collaboration. Mike Wittenstein for his time and expertise. Eric Garland for his intellectual generosity and humor.

And above all, my dad, for encouraging me to think big.

INTRODUCTION: REVOLUTIONS AND REVIVALS

IF YOU EARN YOUR LIVING in the retail industry—and you may not want to hear this—the possibility that the business you're in will still exist in two, five or ten years is very slim. Sorry for the buzzkill, but it's true. In fact, this book may have been more appropriately titled *Surviving* in the new age of consumerism.

If all this sounds overly dramatic, consider some of the brands that (even as I write this) are under deathwatch. By the time you read this, some of these may be gone:

American Airlines, Research In Motion, Pacific Sunwear of California, A&W, Sears, Nokia, American Apparel, Saab, Best Buy, Kmart, RadioShack, Barnes & Noble, Talbots, Suzuki, Avon, AOL, HP, Sony, Yahoo!, Hostess Brands (Twinkies), Kodak, Avery Dennison.

The Mayan calendar aside, the notion that many of these brands could be facing their end, as I write this in 2012, would have seemed beyond credibility only a short time ago. While they're all very differently positioned brands that sell across a range of categories, they also have one thing in common: they each missed or ignored at least one universe-shaping shift in their market, and never quite recovered from it.

For some, the decline has been slow, painful and drawn out. American Airlines, for example, has taken losses of more than $10 billion in the last decade. For others, the descent has been swift. Research In Motion, which was being heralded by *Forbes* in 2009 as the "fastest growing company in the world," has seen its stock in free fall.

What's also worth noting is that the changes these brands failed to adapt to were most often neither subtle nor sudden. They didn't strike like lightning from a clear blue sky. In fact, most were more like slow-motion train wrecks. Avon, for example, missed multiple long-term societal shifts, each of which should have prompted a comprehensive reevaluation of its business model. And Avon wasn't alone. The Sears decline continues to be protracted and painful to watch. Trend after trend sails past, leaving the company in their wake, but, for whatever reason, Sears has failed to take action—or at least the right action to adapt and to survive. It's as if somehow it became stuck in a web of inertia, unable to free itself.

To be fair to both Avon and Sears, it's easy to lose sight of just how rapidly things change, and to suddenly find yourself years, even decades behind. Think about it. As I write this I'm 48 years old, and in my lifetime it was perfectly acceptable for doctors to endorse cigarette brands. One cigar brand—Cigares de Joy—actually promoted itself as medicinal and claimed to provide relief from ailments like sore throat! Small-appliance manufacturer Kenwood advertised that its blender, the Kenwood Chef, "did everything but cook," but hastened to remind us "that's what wives are for." And plus-size fashion retailer Lane Bryant not so long ago produced advertising that referred to their target customers as "Chubbies"! Can you imagine trying to get away with that today? Yet these examples were regarded as perfectly permissible advertising only several short decades ago.

An example of early tobacco advertising claiming the medicinal benefits of smoking.

When I share these examples with audiences, there's almost unanimous agreement on just how completely things have changed in a relatively short period of time, and no one has a problem acknowledging that exponential change has occurred. The funny thing is, when I shift the conversation to the *future* of retail and consumer behavior, and begin to describe some of the significant changes I see on the horizon—even over a short five to ten years hence—I almost always encounter naysayers who are reluctant to buy into the idea that radical change might be around the corner. They find it difficult to imagine that things they do today might become as out of place as doctors hawking cigarettes.

It seems we humans are far more reluctant to accept change when it lies ahead of us than when it's safely in the rearview mirror. And while a healthy dose of skepticism helps us avoid being suckered and taken advantage of, taken to an extreme, habitual skepticism can be lethal. It can interfere with judgment, cause paralysis and ultimately lead an organization to ruin. There is no shortage of examples. Industries filled with brilliant executives have crumbled because of a failure to properly acknowledge the magnitude of the impact that specific changes would have on companies. From the music industry to the video store channel, the business landscape is littered with headstones that read, "We doubted it!"

And this phenomenon is not exclusive to us mere intellectual mortals. Indeed some of the world's most respected minds have similarly underestimated the volume and velocity of change in their markets. In 1933, Boeing predicted that there would never be a plane built that was larger than its 10-seater. Lord William Thomson Kelvin, president of the Royal Society in the late 1800s believed that radio technology would go nowhere and that X-rays would prove to be nothing more than a hoax. And even Bill Gates once said "640K (kilobytes) ought to be enough for anyone."

So, why *do* even incredibly smart people miss what often seem like obvious and devastating changes and trends? It's impossible to know for sure but in my experience working with a diverse mix of private and public organizations, here's what I've observed. It reads a little like the seven deadly sins—except in this case there are 10.

Fear: The organization is so frightened and confused that it becomes petrified and unable to take any action. Instead, it attempts to deny that disruptive change is happening at all. And those people who do attempt to champion change in the organization are often isolated or perhaps even ostracized for it.

Arrogance: The organization perceives that it has such a stranglehold on its suppliers and consumers that it is invincible. Little importance is placed on early detection of future trends, as these organizations regard their past triumphs as proof enough that they can overcome anything on the fly.

Distraction: There is a collective belief that there are simply too many things to get done today to worry about what's going to happen tomorrow. The day-to-day effort of sustaining the organization and its systems leaves little to no time to focus on long-term trends. People in these organizations don't tend to deviate far from their annual objectives and performance plans, despite potentially catastrophic threats to the company.

Apathy: Few people in the organization give a damn about what happens to the business, and most are just waiting to cash out. The best days of the company are behind it and there's simply no energy among employees to conquer any more change. Most just want to play it safe without making waves.

Willful Ignorance: The organization is completely out of step with the disruptive change bearing down on it. It has become completely myopic with respect to what the business does and oblivious to what's happening outside its walls. There is also a tendency among these organizations to believe that the changes occurring in the market somehow apply to everyone *but* them—that they will somehow not be affected.

Lack of Imagination: The organization is unable to foresee what could happen or to *imagine* a different reality, which leads to a paucity of innovation. There is only a small percentage of people who seem to be creative or imaginative enough to construct a clear picture of what *could* be. For most, the future remains a foggy, obscure place, so the tendency is to want to hold on to what's more certain, defined and secure: the present.

Linear versus Exponential Thinking: As humans we tend to project change based on what we see as being the logical extension of our current reality. For example, it seems logical to assume that if cars currently average 25 miles per gallon of gas, that a year or two from now, they will average slightly more than that, owing to better technology. We envision change as being incremental and linear in nature. However, it's essential to understand that when multiple (and often seemingly unrelated) trends intersect, they can result in exponential change. In other words, it's entirely conceivable that two or more trends could intersect resulting in average gas mileage going from 25 mpg to 80 mpg. We see this around us constantly. One isolated medical discovery on one side of the planet may result in new treatments being found for numerous unrelated diseases and conditions somewhere else. Often referred to as Black Swans, these quantum changes are often completely unforeseeable and frequently devastating for businesses.

The Leadership Paradox: The organization looks to its leaders to develop creative solutions to navigating change. The problem is that the most creative people in organizations are very often not perceived to be good leaders and vice versa. The cause, it's believed, could be that creativity often demands unorthodox and radical thinking, whereas leadership is very often more systematic, conservative and rule guided. This means that while the organization may need a complete dismantling of the status quo, its own leaders may actually be perpetuating it!

Old DNA: The organizational mindset is so firmly rooted in the technology, economics and sociology of an earlier era that the leadership simply cannot adapt to the conditions that a new era presents. Despite efforts to adapt, such an anachronistic perspective won't allow the organization to make the transition. Take it from me—nothing is more frustrating than possessing DNA that doesn't match that of the company you're working for. It's excruciating!

Rationalization: Perhaps the deadliest trap of all is the tendency among organizations to simply rationalize change away—to make it seem less critical than it really is. This often takes the form of erroneous comparisons between the current disruption and past challenges that the company has successfully coped with. Companies often make excuses to avoid embracing change. For example, many organizations right now are calling mobile "the new Internet," which gives them a false sense of comfort, rationalizing that because they made it through the Internet era, they can surely survive the transition to mobile. Unfortunately, mobile is *not* the new Internet—any more than hip hop is the new disco—and to treat it as though it were could lead to a plethora of bad decisions.

Perhaps the worst risk in kidding yourself about the future is that you will invariably begin trying to kid your customers into thinking the same way. In 2011, the United States Postal Service (USPS) set about developing media messages that were intended to convince the public to request paper billing statements from their utility companies and other businesses they deal with, as opposed to digital statements. After all, with consumers moving most of their banking and other payments online, the market for mail delivery was taking it on the chin. From a business standpoint, the urgency to recoup this lost revenue made perfect sense. But here's where things went wrong—rather than trying to invent a new and transformative model for bill payment that USPS could own a stake in and that customers would love, it decided instead to treat the public like complete idiots.

This culminated in a strategy (if I can call it that) involving a TV commercial portraying delighted customers opening mailed paper statements and proudly sticking them to their fridge or office corkboard. The accompanying narrative cheerfully proclaimed, "A refrigerator has never been hacked. An online virus has never attacked a corkboard. Give your customers the added feeling of security a printed statement or receipt provides, with mail. It's good for business and even better for your customers."

 Scan this to watch the USPS commercial. (If you need a smartphone app that scans QR codes, go to getscanlife.com on your mobile device.)

The commercial went viral, but unfortunately for the USPS, it did so for all the wrong reasons. It got passed around the Internet as a farcical example of an organization that had its head in the sand and was trying to bury its customers' heads there with it. One couldn't help wondering if the USPS might not also be considering a follow-up campaign to resurrect the pony express!

Regrettably, the Postal Service isn't the only organization wasting time with such inane tactics. The bookstore channel has gone to great lengths in its attempt to convince us that deep down we all still love the smell and feel of paper books, when every available statistic suggests that we actually prefer the smell and feel of tablets and e-readers. The music industry has invested millions to make us believe that the world will fly off its axis if we share songs with friends, while even recording artists themselves are moving on and developing new, imaginative ways—beyond record sales—to create revenue *and* happy fans. Cable providers continue to screw customers into buying packaged programming at ridiculous costs, while increasing numbers of viewers cut their cable cords and move to streamed online alternatives.

In the end, what all these defensive countermeasures amount to is a colossal waste of time. Time that companies *could* have and *should* have spent creating new platforms, new concepts and new models for their category—which they (and not Apple, Amazon or Google) could own!

So the first and perhaps the most important step is actually *accepting* that radical change is indeed real and happening, and that it will, at some point, touch your business, if it hasn't already. Disruption is inevitable.

"Speed has never killed anyone. Suddenly becoming stationary, that's what gets you."
—*Jeremy Clarkson, Host of BBC's Top Gear*

Once you've come to terms with the magnitude of the changes taking place in the retail industry, it's important to understand the *speed* at which these things are unfolding. Business innovation is moving exponentially faster today than at any other time in history. To put an exclamation mark on this, I've been asking audiences that I speak to how many had heard of the photo app Instagram—*before* hearing that Facebook purchased the company for a billion dollars. Most people had not heard of the company before that point, and, in fact, some had never heard of Instagram at all, even *after* Facebook bought it. To fully comprehend the significance of the Instagram example, consider that at one point in my career I worked for a company that required 123 years to achieve a billion dollars in annual revenue, and required well over a thousand employees, multiple manufacturing sites and operations in two countries to do it. Instagram achieved a market value of a billion dollars (at least on paper) in two years and with a dozen staff. In fact, within 10 days of the acquisition by Facebook, Instagram added an additional 10 million users! That's how quickly things are moving today.

This really screws up the fast-follow strategy that so many companies have slyly prided themselves on executing for so long. (Let someone else take the risk, the expense and the misfires, and only come on board once the concept is proven.) This simply won't work anymore—things are moving too fast and that means you have to go first in your category if you plan to go at all. You have to live way out on the edge of what's happening and experiment constantly with new things well before they're proven. Your company—not someone else's—has to accept the risk and uncertainty.

So make no mistake: everything you're seeing today is new—you've never been here before. It's all unfamiliar ground. Sure, you can *infer* some things here and there based on experience, but you can't assume that the approach you used yesterday will be effective today. Doing so is a recipe for disaster.

To put it simply, there has been no other point in history when so many aspects of disruptive change have collided and conspired to wreak havoc on the retail and consumer packaged goods industries. Every facet of how things are produced, brought to market, merchandised and ultimately sold to consumers is being challenged, tested and eradicated. Who the customer is, what customers want and how to give it to them are completely up for grabs. Our entire concept of what a store *is* is being entirely transformed.

This is, all at once, the most exhilarating, electrifying and terrifying time in the history of consumerism!

And, as transfixed as we've all become by the global economy, I think you'll see that this is hardly all about economics. Not by a long shot! If anything, the economic volatility of the last five or six years has been a *distraction* from other deeper, broader and more permanent shifts in our society. What the retail industry is experiencing now (and going forward) is not merely an economic speed bump—it's a head-on, no-airbag crash into the end of multiple eras, some stretching back as far as 2,000 years! So if you're still waiting for the "bounce-back," take a seat—it's not going to happen. In fact, the elephant in the room is that there is no "recovery," contrary to what many of us would like to think. This is permanent. It's the end of one era and the beginning of a new one. My hope is that this book will help you not only understand it, but thrive in it.

I should also tell you now that this book is not intended to be a highly academic treatise on retail and consumer behavior. This exciting industry doesn't need another dreadful book that makes the industry seem boring. It's also not intended to be a data-dump of statistics and facts meant to overwhelm or scare you. If anything, that's the problem with most of the information that's thrown at us on a day-to-day basis. It's sensational, loosely researched, lacks context and frightens the hell out of us. What it doesn't do is help us get on with it—to do what we do better, and to create better consumer experiences.

Unfortunately, most retail-industry trade associations aren't helping much either. To my continual amazement, most associations seem to shy away from the really tough conversations—the stuff their members may not want to hear but need to know.

So, my humble aim here is to shine a bright light on all the scary things you hear moving under your company's bed: the really big, ugly megatrends that go bump in the night. Above all, I want to share the unprecedented opportunities that lie ahead to create better, more fulfilling retail experiences for consumers, retailers and brands.

If we're being honest with ourselves, retail has sucked for the last few decades. In fact, I'm confident that history will regard the last 30 years as retail's dark ages, a time when the joy of shopping was kicked aside by mindless, credit-crazed consumption. A time when the success of a retailer was more often measured by its scale of operations and share value than by its product quality, shopping experience or positive impact on society. This was a time when the term *customer service* became so overused and trite that it lost all value and meaning. We treated people and machines as though they were interchangeable and, in the process, we made both largely ineffective and indifferent to customers. We built enormous, soulless concrete boxes, filled them with junk and called the result "power retail" to legitimize it and make it sound somehow noble. Meanwhile, working in retail became something people did only until they found a *real* job. Retail workers were given more drudgery, static pay rates and less mobility. To use the phrase made famous by Walmart founder Sam Walton, we "stacked it high and watched it fly" and, in doing so, lost much of the social value and benefit that retail can have in a society.

Here's a test. The next time you're at a shopping mall, take a look at the directory and ask yourself how many of the retailers on the list you'd actually miss if they disappeared tomorrow. As you drive to work, count the stores along the way that you feel an emotional attachment to. Open your fridge and add up the products inside that you feel are simply irreplaceable. If you need to count them on more than one hand, I'd be amazed. The unfortunate truth is that many of the retailers and brands hanging on today have managed to do so because we consumers were spending unprecedented piles of borrowed money. We would have bought sand at the beach! Well, that period is over now, the credit well is dry and it's time once again to actually *earn* a place in consumers' hearts and minds by giving them something remarkable and worthy of their attention.

All of this amounts to what I see as a fantastic revival. A revival for manufacturers, retailers and consumers alike—a rebirth of sorts, and a return to what makes retailing wonderful. I'm convinced that all this tumult will ultimately create a better retail marketplace, where deserving companies can shine and consumers can enjoy infinitely better experiences; a place where talented people can once again earn a gainful living and perform meaningful, exciting work. After all, when it's done right, shopping is social, personal and fun. How we shop is a direct reflection of societal values—an integral part of who we are. We have lost sight of that over the last 30 years.

This is very good news for those companies that have the courage, inspiration and conviction to succeed in the new era of consumerism. It's also a wonderful new age for marketers who aspire to create remarkable, memorable experiences that make a difference in people's lives. Most of all, it's tremendous news for consumers who, after decades of covetous consumption, long to rediscover the true magic of shopping.

Make no mistake about it: the golden age of retail lies stretched out before us. How we shop will change more in the next 20 years than it did in the previous 1,000.

Vive la revival!

Part 1

The End

1

It's Not a "Recession"!

IN THE SPRING OF 2006, I was asked to lunch by the president of a major North American paint manufacturing company. The company had done outstandingly well over the last three decades or so, selling its products through independent retail outlets across the United States and Canada. So well, in fact, that many of the dealers had become unimaginably wealthy in the process. You might be dubious that one could get rich selling house paint, but that's exactly what had happened and was still happening with a fair degree of regularity. The owners of these paint stores were buying vacation properties in exclusive 'hoods such as Palm Beach, Florida, Salt Spring Island, B.C., and Scottsdale, Arizona. It seemed that they were all making money faster than they could spend it.

It wasn't unusual for this paint manufacturer to wine and dine its dealers at some of the most exclusive resorts in North America. Dealers were offered five-star meals, Cuban cigars and the finest single-malt Scotches. It was all strangely

3

surreal. On this particular day, the company president had selected a very nice restaurant on New York's Upper East Side. Being a Manhattanite himself, he frequented many of the best restaurants in the city. Over lunch we came to talk about one dealer in particular—a family-owned operation based in Manhattan and Long Island that had done astonishingly well. The dealer, founded in the 1800s, had a long history. What, for most of its existence, had been a grimy little New York paint operation, became a well-oiled money machine by the early 2000s. Indeed, by 2005, with only a handful of often tiny, nondescript stores, the business was closing in on $100 million in sales. Its performance was nothing short of amazing.

The paint company's president was making the point to me that this particular dealer had been especially skillful in developing its business. He pointed to several innovations that he felt had largely fueled the dealer's success: modifications to its stores, new displays and new methods of selling, etcetera. The dealer was, in the president's estimation, a retail genius. At this point I (perhaps wrongly) interjected, countering that in addition to all the sensible and well-executed steps the dealer and his staff had taken with their business, they'd also gotten extremely lucky. I offered that given the unprecedented social and economic conditions of the late twentieth century, it would, in fact, have been very difficult for the dealer *not* to succeed. Being located in New York, I added, only helped to amplify the dealer's gains. All this was not to say that the dealer couldn't have failed along the way—some of its competitors certainly had. However, all other things being equal, the deck was so tremendously stacked in the paint dealer's favor that, short of doing something really stupid, it couldn't lose. Its success, I maintained, was ultimately as much a product of fortunate circumstance as it was prescience or extraordinary skill.

In that instant, it was as if all the air in the room had been suddenly sucked out. The president was very obviously disturbed that I would suggest that dumb luck and not superior business savvy could be at the heart of his top retailer's outstanding success. "How could you suggest such a thing?" he asked, with a look in his eyes that said, "I hope you choke on your salad!" Clearly he took my comments as an insinuation that the last few decades in business had been some sort of cake-walk! It was as though he believed I was demeaning the business and financial achievements of an entire generation — my own included!

And he was absolutely right.

———

Fast-forward ...

In September 2010, the U.S. National Bureau of Economic Research stated that the "recession," which this august body declared officially over in June of that year, was indeed the longest on record since World War II. Although history books will record its official duration as two years, it has really been almost six years since the show began, and it's clearly not over yet. Let's put that into perspective. If you had a child who was 12 when the shit hit the fan, he or she is now just about old enough to vote. Barack Obama was an Illinois senator when Wall Street crumbled. He's now (as I write this) preparing to begin his second term as president — and still struggling to right the economic situation. Since 2009, the retail industry in particular has been on what has become a week-to-week roller-coaster ride of global economic upset, from anemic domestic consumer demand to the black hole that is the European debt crisis to clear signs that the once-unstoppable economic force of China is now indeed weakening (albeit to what are still enviable levels of growth). Every week it seems that there's a new economic, technological or social headwind pushing retail off course. The consumer economy we knew in North America has become like a patient on life support, with analysts, retailers and brands

all gathered at its bedside searching for any sign of life—
the blink of an eye, the twitch of a finger, anything! Monthly
industry results have become as ominous as an EKG, showing a faint and erratic heartbeat, fluctuating between signs of
hope and despair.

Perhaps most troubling is that many in the retail industry
still appear to be holding out for a clean recovery—a point
at which they can simply dust themselves off and get back to
business as usual. In fact, I often hear executives comment-
ing on their business in terms of whether it appears to be
"coming back" or "not coming back." But the question that
most seem unable to answer is: Coming back to *what*? What
are we hoping to return to? Far from projecting the future
of their businesses, many of the corporate leadership teams
that I speak to have yet to even fully come to an agreement
on what exactly caused this disaster in the first place. It's
as though they were flying along the highway enjoying the
scenery, when all of a sudden they crashed into something!
The problem is that they had no idea what they hit or how
much damage was done; they just knew that now something
was terribly wrong. And their real troubles started when,
instead of pulling over to properly assess the wreckage, they
just carried on, trying to get back up to speed. The trouble
being, of course, that they couldn't.

"Study the past, if you would divine the future."
— *Confucius*

The unsettling truth is that the *comeback*, which many are
hoping for, will never happen. Just as the Spanish explorer
Hernán Cortés scuttled his ships upon arriving in Mexico,
we too are stuck in this strange, foreign consumer landscape.
There's no going back and we'd better start learning how to
deal with it. The economic, social and technological change
we're experiencing now is not a mere recession but rather
the beginning of something entirely new and uncharted.

Call it the new normal, call it, as author Brian Solis put it, "the end of business as usual," call it whatever you want, but know that it is *not* going to go away. In fact, the current economic event has only been the catalyst for other, deeper changes in consumer behavior, many of which likely would have occurred anyway, but were hastened along and significantly compounded by the economic downturn. This goes much deeper than being a recession—this is indeed, as General Electric's (GE's) Jeff Immelt said, a complete "emotional, social, economic reset."[1] It is a reset of our entire consumer economy. Perhaps the only way to fully understand this is by trying to answer a few simple questions. They are:

- How, in less than 34 years, did a local Atlanta lumber store, called the Home Depot become a global chain of over 3,000 locations with an average store size of 100,000 square feet (in total, 300 million square feet of hardware)?

- How did Best Buy, a Minnesota electronics retailer go from selling one million dollars' worth of goods in 1970 to over a billion in 1992, and then experience a sharp rise in sales to $16.55 billion in 2010?

- How, in 50 short years, did Sam Walton's five-and-dime store grow to become larger than the economy of Sweden and employ more people than the entire population of Paris?

How was it exactly that these retailers and countless others experienced such unimaginable growth in such a short period of time? How did *they* grow so exponentially when the overall rate of economic growth in the United States since 1946 has been between 3 percent and 3.5 percent? Perhaps if we understand precisely why that happened in the first place, it will give us some insight into why it's coming to an abrupt end and why it simply can't happen again.

But first, humor me. Take a moment, close your eyes and think about your own business, regardless of what business you're in. What if I told you that I could grant you two things? For starters, I could deliver to you a steady and ever-growing stream of customers, all of whom have better earning potential than your current customers. Secondly, I could promise you that the needs and preferences of these customers would be narrow enough in breadth that you could satisfy them with a fairly tight assortment of goods and services. How would that be? Lots of new customers, all of whom want basically the same narrow selection? Of course, there isn't a business on earth that wouldn't kill for those sorts of optimal conditions. But that's the thing: if you were in retail in the 1960s, you didn't have to kill anyone. You had these exact circumstances delivered to you—by the stork!

WHERE WERE YOU IN '62?

In early 2012, I got a call from *Advertising Age* magazine. The editors were doing a special edition of the magazine commemorating the 50th anniversary of Kmart, Walmart, Kohl's and Target. It seems that each of these brands began life in 1962, and the editor wanted to know if I could contribute a piece projecting what the next 50 years might hold for them and for the big-box retail format in general.

I couldn't help being struck by the fact that four of America's most formidable discount department stores all happened to share a 1962 birth date. Was this just mere coincidence? I wondered. Of course, it was no mystery that the baby boom was a driving force behind retail growth. If these brands had had their respective starts at various points throughout the decade, it wouldn't have been a surprise at all. But they all came about in *exactly the same year*! I wondered what was so special about that particular year that it spawned these four behemoth retailers—one of whom (Walmart) became the world's largest. What was it exactly about 1962 that was so damn good?

To satisfy my curiosity, I began exploring the date of origin for other brands from the same era. Here's where it gets interesting. My research proceeded like the plot of a detective novel. The more I investigated, the more suspects steadily began surfacing—brands that were also tied to the same 1962 date of origin. The year, it seemed, was significant not only to department stores, but to merchants of all categories and formats. And when I expanded the search to include the period from 1961 to 1969, the list became a veritable who's who of consumer brands and chains across just about every category of goods and services imaginable, and included names from around the world! Here are only some of the more notable brands I found:

- Arthur Treacher's Fish and Chips (1969)
- B&Q (UK) (1969)
- Bank of America Home Loans (1969)
- Best Buy (1966)
- Calvin Klein (1968)
- Crate and Barrel (1962)
- Frito-Lay (1961)
- Gap (1969)
- Home Hardware (1964)
- Hyundai (1967)
- JanSport (1967)
- K-Swiss (1966)
- K-tel (1968)
- Lands' End (1963)
- Limited Brands (1963)
- Little Tikes (1969)

- Long John Silver's (1969)
- Mac's Convenience Stores (1962)
- Mary Kay (1963)
- MasterCard (1966)
- Norwegian Cruise Line (1966)
- Peet's Coffee & Tea (1966)
- PepsiCo (1965)
- Petco (1965)
- Pier 1 Imports (1962)
- Princess Cruises (1965)
- Rite Aid (1962)
- Roy Rogers Restaurants (1968)
- Safeway (UK) (1962)
- *Sesame Street* (1969)
- Six Flags Over Texas (1961)
- The Children's Place (1969)
- The North Face (1966)
- Toll Brothers (1967)
- TOPS Markets (1962)
- Topshop (1964)
- Vans (1966)
- Wendy's Old Fashioned Hamburgers (1969)
- Woolco (1962)
- Yves Saint Laurent (1962)

I discovered that even businesses like McDonald's, founded in the late 1940s, experienced their most astonishing growth from 1962 onward. In fact, 1963 saw the chain's inception of clown mascot Ronald McDonald, an idea credited to McDonald's owner Ray Kroc, who had purchased the company one year earlier from the McDonald brothers. You might wonder, why incorporate a clown as your mascot? And why the early 1960s connection again? As I would find out, the answer is simple mathematics.

 Scan this to watch McDonald's first-ever TV commercial with Ronald McDonald here. Warning: It's a little weird!

MORE! AND MORE! AND MORE!

David Foot and Daniel Stoffman's seminal 1996 book *Boom, Bust & Echo* put into crisp focus the impact that baby boomers had and would have on our economy. There isn't a business in North America that hasn't in some way been influenced by what was an absolutely unprecedented wave of population growth. Although the timeline is sometimes debated, most agree that the baby boom truly began in 1946 and lasted until 1964. To put the magnitude of the boom into perspective, in the years following World War II, mothers experienced fertility rates that were up to 30 percent higher than they were before the war began—a mind-boggling increase, and one that would ultimately fuel economic growth for many years to come. What fewer people might realize, however, is that the actual peak year for the live birth number in the United States was in fact 1957— 11 years after the beginning of the boom. It was only after a strong surge in live birth numbers in 1947, and a subsequent drop until 1950, that the birth rate began steadily increasing in 1951, hitting an all-time high in 1957. From 1957 to 1961 the rate essentially plateaued and then began to decline again around 1962.

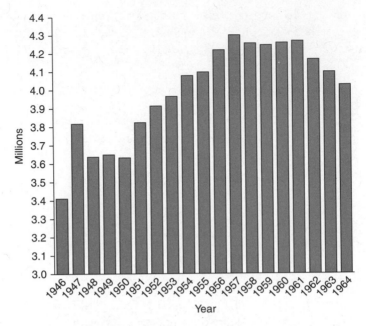

Source: Bureau of Labor Statistics, U.S. census data

No one could have known it at the time, but it was during these unusually strong birth years (1951 to 1957) that the foundation of seemingly boundless opportunity was being laid for retailers and brands. Wages were increasing, jobs were secure and American families were hungry for all the trappings of one of the nation's most embedded cultural paradigms: the middle-class life. In each of those seven years, the number of live births escalated well above the norm, and, as you'd expect, the impact on businesses in every category was profound! By 1962, the challenge for retail was simply keeping up with excess demand. This massive initial swell of baby boomers were now between 5 and 16 years old, and by virtue of their sheer numbers, needed more of everything: more shirts, shoes and bikes; more trips to Disneyland; more cheeseburgers; and more cartoons. More! More! More!

And *more* was precisely what they got. Malls and strip plazas popped up like weeds in towns across America. In fact, between 1960 and 1970 more than 8,000 malls were built! That is double the pace of development set through the 1950s. Then, with the advent of temperature-controlled malls and nighttime shopping, Americans could shop whenever they liked in complete comfort. Malls became increasingly larger, evolving to become two and three stories in an effort to meet the needs of an ever-expanding universe of merchants who were rushing to serve armies of consumers. The retail industry as a whole went into a maniacal state of overdrive to accommodate the boom in population and prosperity.[2]

The explosive pace of development continued for decades. And as this crescendo of the boom passed through the economy, the only things that changed from one decade to the next were the categories of products and services that were created to satiate the demands of the baby boomer children as they grew into young adults. You didn't have to be a marketing guru or operational genius to do well under these circumstances. With a reasonably convenient store location and a good supply of decent products, you could make money. If you added some business savvy and a strong work ethic into the mix, you could make a fortune and many did! As Philip Kotler points out in his book *The Principles of Marketing*, as a result of the boom "Levi-Strauss & Co. and other jeans makers experienced heady 10–15 per cent annual sales growth [through the 1960s and 1970s], with little or no strategic or marketing planning effort. Selling jeans was easy—Levi concentrated on simply trying to make enough jeans to satisfy a seemingly insatiable market."

There was no question that by 1962 a tipping point had been reached. The surf was up on what was the largest single wave of population growth in U.S. history, and brands like Walmart, Kmart, Kohl's and Target grabbed their boards!

CHOCOLATE OR VANILLA?

If the explosion in the consumer population wasn't cause enough for celebration, these new consumers also happened to share remarkably similar tastes and preferences. They basically liked the same stuff! Of course there may have been nuances here and there to meet circumstances of geography and income, but, broadly speaking, consumers were extremely similar in lifestyle, family composition and ethnic background. They were, on balance, white, middle-class children from two-parent, single-income homes.

Even immigration to the United States and Canada leading up to the mid-1960s was largely homogeneous. The United States and Canada were "white-settler" countries, and immigrants to these nations largely arrived from the UK and some other parts of continental Europe. It wasn't until the mid-1960s, when the "racial preference" language was removed from the immigration policies of both countries, that the nationalities of newcomers began to diversify significantly. The homogeneity of the 1960's market made identifying and projecting customer needs, tastes and preferences remarkably straightforward by today's standards. Flavors, colors, prints, patterns and styles were all fairly simple to select if you happened to be a buyer for Target. This ability to accurately project consumer preferences meant that large chains could comfortably count on selling through large quantities of inventory over several months to a year or more and not have to worry about changing up the mix. This in turn meant they could buy in bulk at sharp prices, sell across a narrow range of SKUs and discount prices at retail sufficiently to keep customers coming back for more. And for those rare needs that a retailer couldn't or didn't want to satisfy with its usual stock, the retailer could always rely on catalog sales or special orders—after all, consumers had very few alternatives when it came to getting what they wanted. In other words, for a retailer, this was paradise!

In terms of market positioning, *thrift* was a message that sat well with households raising large families on one salary, and people like Sam Walton knew it. There was nothing complex or heady about the marketing message that Walton and others crafted. It was a clean, pure message that resonated with families of the 1960s, many of whom still had wartime spending restraint firmly entrenched in their psyches. In fact, many of their children (leading-edge baby boomers) were still being taught the value of saving money in school through programs like the postal savings stamps program, which continued into the early 1960s, allowing kids to collect stamps that were redeemable for savings bonds. Thrift was a surefire winning message. So, with the average American shopper squarely in its sights, the first Walmart store opened in 1962 with a simple four-word tagline emblazoned on its signage. These four words would come to define an unprecedented era in retail: WE SELL FOR LESS. But the 1960s were a mere dress rehearsal for what awaited.

THE INDUSTRIAL DEVOLUTION

As the baby boomers joined the workforce, married and had children of their own, they paved the way for what would come to be known as the suburban power center and the era of the big-box. Main Street store formats (or, as British immigrants would still call them, the shops along "high street") did not have the capacity to serve the demands of the massive generation that was just embarking on its prime spending years. Stores swelled to the size of football stadiums, carrying every product known to man. The sheer gravitational pull of power centers laid to ruin most of the continent's Main Street retail shops. The vast majority of small- and medium-size merchants were annihilated, swallowed whole or simply forgotten in the frenzy.

Little did we know that what we were witnessing (and contributing to) was the *industrialization of retail*: the exact point at which retailing ceased to be a craft and instead became an occupation. The new era would bear witness to the displacement of personal service, unique products and artful merchandising by stack-outs, blowouts and rollbacks. Quality would take a back seat to availability, and abundance would triumph over substance. Throughout the 1980s the big-box formula for domination was invincible and dauntingly repeatable. Commercial developers and large chains simply identified growth markets for residential development, built their stores on the commercial fringe of that development and waited a year or so for consumers to come. And by God they did! Like moths to a flame, shoppers flocked to them. Because in a pre-Internet, world nothing could top the mind-blowing selection, prices and convenience of the big-box store. The big-box was a wonder!

But that wasn't all. It was also around this time that the U.S. federal government, which had long advocated economic sobriety and encouraged consumers to save their money, abruptly began aggressively promoting higher levels of consumer spending and borrowing as the surest path to the country's economic prosperity. And as any economist will tell you, the real estate market is one of the best catalysts for stimulating the circulation of cash. Unfortunately, in the government's zeal to allow a free flow of cash in the economy, a series of bipartisan economic policy decisions that were made through the 1980s and into the early 2000s actually resulted in banks providing mortgages to less-than-qualified (or, subprime) homeowners (several million mortgages, in fact). These subprime mortgages facilitated millions of home purchases, which, before that time, would never have happened. This increased sales volume drove the real estate market into a frenzy. And because the government had removed the regulatory firewall between the investment and retail banking sectors, the banks were able to bundle up all these newly minted mortgages and sell them to investment firms. The investment firms in turn sold them to their clients under the harmless-sounding moniker *mortgage-backed assets*—often carrying bogus triple-A ratings. With home prices escalating at an unprecedented pace, many Americans, encouraged by their lenders, succumbed to the temptation to use their home as a *live-in credit card*. This helped to subsidize household income, which had remained stubbornly stagnant through the same period. So, even though average Americans weren't actually earning more money, this rising well of home-equity borrowing made them feel as though they were managing. As a consequence, the household debt-to-income ratio redlined at almost 140 and the personal savings rate plummeted to almost nil. But no one cared. Everyone was living like a rock star! In fact, between 1980 and 2005 the U.S. economy grew by an incredible 100 percent, led by an army of baby boomers in the prime of their consumer lives. It was like one big toga party!

And then the unthinkable happened. As homeowners who couldn't afford their mortgages in the first place began to default on payments, stock of repossessed homes rose and the market became choked with inventory. Real estate values dropped like a rock, which in turn caused even more defaults. Soon, even those homeowners who *could* afford their mortgages began to walk away from homes where the value had fallen below outstanding loan balances. This crushed market values further—and so it went, on and on.

When all was said and done, the worst-hit markets saw home values decrease by over 50 percent. Consequently, all those nice little bundles of mortgages that Wall Street companies were peddling became worthless and caused even enormous investment firms and banks to implode. With these major institutions now falling into insolvency, the markets took a steep dive, removing over $10 trillion (with a *T*) in wealth from the wallets and bank accounts of Americans alone—many of whom were depending on that money for their retirement. The entire economic house of cards, which had taken well over two decades to construct, had toppled, leaving most of the developed world in a state of absolute shock.

As one would expect, consumers took to the root cellar in a swift and certain flight to frugality, declaring a lockdown on spending through most of 2009. Since then, the industry has kept a daily vigil over consumers, waiting for any sustained signs of recovery.

And that, I'm afraid, is where the fairy tale ends. The magical set of circumstances that gave rise to 50 years of unprecedented consumption has run its course, and we now find ourselves confronting much more than what some still refer to as "just a recession." This animal is far more complex than a mere dip or cycle in economic activity. Rather, what we're reckoning with now is a complete reversal of the circumstances that brought us to this point in the first place. It is the end of something easy and the beginning of something much more difficult.

SCORCHED EARTH

Today, 50 years after the wave of 1960s consumption began, the very youngest baby boomers are 49 years old. According to the U.S. Bureau of Labor Statistics, it is a statistical certainty that spending among Americans begins to decline after the age of 50. We simply need less stuff once we reach 50 and beyond. In fact, most of us by that age are trying to pawn our junk off on our kids! This natural decline in spending typically comes gradually as a generation ages. What's happened, however, has been a more abrupt shutting off of the tap as boomers, many of whom lost ground in the stock and real estate markets, begin to reevaluate their situations. Many have found themselves standing at the edge of the precipice of retirement without a parachute.

Statistics aside, some would argue that boomers are still the wealthiest generation in history, and that their spending won't simply dry up, but will merely shift away from certain categories like electronics and housewares and toward others like travel and health services. And while this shift is already taking place, there are other issues that are only now beginning to surface. One is that baby boomers are carrying record debt loads. Some of this debt resulted from refinancing real estate for other major purchases, paying for the kids' college tuition and assisting parents who were becoming infirm. In other cases, unforeseen medical expenses were to blame. Regardless of the cause, what is clear is that, at a time in their lives when boomers should have been squirreling money away, they were borrowing more.

So, while it is true that certain categories will experience monumental growth over the next 40 years as boomers continue to age, the economy as a whole will have to find a new workhorse. Boomers, for all intents and purposes, are done.

Taking up the mantle of consumerism for them is Generation X, the generation born between 1965 and 1984. The problem is that even by the most conservative estimates this generation is at least 15 percent smaller than the baby boomer generation, and hence is often referred to as the "baby bust." The generation's relatively small size, coupled with the rockier economic conditions that Gen Xers have faced throughout much of their work lives, have resulted in financial challenges. They have been deprived of many of the opportunities that boomers enjoyed, and now they suffer, waiting (im)patiently for their boomer bosses to retire. But it looks like that could be a while. In fact, in 2012, the percentage of the workforce working past age 65 hit an all-time high. All of this means more lost time (and opportunity) for Gen X. There should probably be a day each year where boomers send cards to Gen X to formally say they're sorry! Sorry for taking all the best jobs and making all the money before the music stopped.

Some argue, however, that Generation X may actually end up being the beneficiary of a colossal talent crisis as boomers leave the workforce over the next 20 years and the market struggles with small numbers of qualified candidates to take their place. However, one could easily argue that a large percentage of the jobs that boomers occupy today will be eliminated in 10 years anyway; they will either be eliminated by technology or be outsourced. And I have to agree; many of these jobs are unnecessary today. For those reasons, I don't foresee the impending talent shortage that some do. So, short of arming the generation with limitless credit cards, the idea of Generation X saving the economy is actually somewhat of a mathematical impossibility. They simply cannot (and will not) spend with the same veracity that boomers did. And perhaps that's a good thing. That leaves Generation Y, or the Millennial Generation (as they're sometimes called).

Compared to Generation X, Gen Y is a huge generational cohort that has become almost mythical for its consumer prowess. By the mid 2000s, it was hard to attend a retailing conference that didn't have a number of workshops on how to tap this high-value consumer cohort—a cohort that was, by the numbers, spending 500 percent more than their parents did at the same age. By most accounts, members of Gen Y had more discretionary income than their parents, and were gaining an unusually early appetite for the finer things in life. And even if they weren't the ones making the purchase directly, they appeared to influence family buying patterns on everything from peanut butter to Porsches.

Gen Y, it seemed, was the one great hope for the economy. Regrettably, even the fortunes of Generation Y have not played out as hoped. In reality, Millennials appear to be caught in a crisis of their own. Because many of the generation's parents found it difficult to fund their children's educations, many Gen Y kids have had little choice but to borrow. According to American Student Assistance, in 2007–2008 lenders loaned $19 billion in private student loans—an increase of 592 percent from a decade earlier. In fact, in each school year between 2000–2001 and 2006–2007, an estimated 60 percent of bachelor's degree recipients borrowed to fund their education. During the same time period, average debt per borrower rose 18 percent, from $19,300 to $22,700.

Perhaps even more frightening is that by 2008, half of all college students were carrying four or more credit cards and carrying record-high balances. But the most ominous of all is that a growing percentage of these loans are non-federal private loans by many of the same companies that were implicated in the subprime crisis.

The reality is that an alarming number of students are graduating with what amounts to small mortgages before they even begin working. And work is hard to come by—fully 50 percent of all American students graduating today with a bachelor's degree will find themselves unemployed or underemployed. It's a national crisis that could cause a decades-long hangover for us all.

THE REVIVAL

So, the unfortunate news for retailers is that this is by no means a mere recession. There is no neat and tidy recovery around the corner. There is no natural heir apparent to the baby boomer consumer. There is no one easily targetable group like the baby boomers out there to sell to. And unlike during the 1960s, there's no big fat homogenous segment in today's market. It just doesn't exist. The prototypical household that represented the big bull's-eye in the market is an increasing minority. In fact, today's consumer market comprises a myriad of lifestyles, family compositions, ethnic backgrounds and economic standings, and all of it seems to amount to less direct influence on who buys what. Identifying your "ideal target consumer" in this landscape is, as one of my most loved bosses used to say, like trying to "pick fly shit out of pepper." In other words, it's really hard!

What's making it even harder is that consumer attitudes, too, are in a state of flux. The fallout of 2008 has given us all reason to pause and take stock of our lifestyles, needs and economic frailty. For some this has meant cutting back a little here and there. For others it has represented a wholesale change in the way they live. Even the tools we're using to measure our progress seem oddly antiquated in today's economy. The Consumer Confidence Index (instituted in the relative stability of 1967 for example, seems out of place today, in a world where catastrophic economic change can sweep from one side of the globe to the other in a matter of hours. Can consumers really be expected to project their future economic circumstances in a world moving so quickly? If our central bankers are unable to do so, how can the average consumer? Can they even be certain about their current state in a landscape that's shifting so dramatically?

In 2011, I interviewed author and social theorist John Gerzema, who had recently released his latest book entitled *Spend Shift*, which he coauthored with Michael D'Antonio. *Spend Shift* chronicles what John and Michael perceived as historic shifts in consumer behavior in the days following the 2008 financial crisis. In what he terms "the great unwind," John described to me what he sees as a hopeful horizon where consumers actually *take back* control of their behavior, holding themselves and the companies they do business with to higher business and social standards. It will be a time when responsible purchasing can mitigate the rampant consumerism that marked the boomer decades. His research pointed to a consumer who had become infinitely more mindful and considered in his or her purchasing behavior, and who had begun to anchor his or her brand choices to starkly different values than years past. The more traditionally sought-after brand attributes of convenience, selection and price had begun, he found, to give way to new and deeper qualities like kindness, empathy and lasting quality. Consumers, it seemed, longed to return to a time when they could actually *like* the places they shopped and feel good about spending their money there.

There was one thing in particular from our conversation, though, that really stuck with me. John stated that while many were calling this post-crisis economic climate the *new normal*, he actually saw it as being the *old normal*. In John's mind, it was the last 50 years that were really more of an anomaly, relative to consumer behavior throughout the rest of history. This recession, in other words, wasn't causing a hiatus from consumerism; rather, it was reforming consumerism back to how it was intended to be: thoughtful, responsible and values based. Our very concept of capitalism, as he saw it, was shifting from being about consumers' desire for *more* to their preference for *better*.

For my part, I believe this is not a recovery at all but rather a revival—a revival of our values as consumers, our businesses as retailers and brands and a complete rethink of how the two harmonize in an entirely new era of consumerism. And unlike the recovery, which was spasmodic at best, the revival appears to be well underway and gathering steam—and brands that didn't sit idly by waiting for a recovery are leading the charge. Yoga and athletic apparel retailer Lululemon Athletica, for example, continues to take North America by storm. Nordstrom continues to post solid results and even in the darkest days of the recession, Apple still has a knack for getting massive crowds into its stores. While they are each very different companies, they have one important thing in common: a distinct and "own-able" position in their market based not on *mass*, but on *meaning*. For Lululemon it's an inspiring brand culture built around Eastern philosophy and yoga as a way of life. For Nordstrom it's an unwavering belief in quality service and the value of superior, transformative experiences, and for Apple it's about providing a place for people who want desperately to believe that they too are a little "different." Each of these organizations is as much a community as they are a brand or, as author Seth Godin might put it, a "tribe" unto themselves. These brands understand that they can no longer simply ride a rising tide of population, credit and frenzied consumption. There is no excess, captive demand out there. Those days are gone. There's also no free pass to the future—in fact, the price of admission is extremely steep.

The brands that secure their place in the future will ultimately have to be trusted and loved—and above all, remarkable.

2

The Disappearing Middle

A GOOD PART OF MY CHILDHOOD was spent in the aisles of our local Sears department store; in fact, very few weeks passed without at least one visit. My parents liked it there. They liked the quality, the prices and, above all, the customer satisfaction guarantee. If you decided to return something that you'd purchased at Sears, you simply took it back for a full refund—no questions asked. On the trust scale, I suspect that my parents would have positioned Sears somewhere between God and the Pope (and the Pope would have run a distant third). Consequently, my childhood home was a suburban shrine to the Kenmore and Craftsman brands, and beyond tools and appliances, much of what we owned came from a Sears store.

For my family and so many others, Sears and other similar mid-tier chains were the centers of the consumer universe. These chains were the product of an unprecedented economic phenomenon and were, in essence, the trading posts of middle-class life.

"The most perfect political community is one in which the middle class is in control, and outnumbers both of the other classes."

—*Aristotle*

LIFE IN MIDDLE-EARTH

Perhaps no other socioeconomic concept is as foundational to North American culture as that of the middle class. So much of our collective ethos around equity, prosperity and quality of life is anchored to this formative ideology. Just ask 10 people on the street which class they belong to and, inevitably, most will say the middle class—whether they do or not. To most, the very idea of democracy as a way of life is inextricably tied to a strong and growing middle class.

Ironically, despite how intrinsic the middle-class ideal has become to developed societies, there's surprisingly little alignment among economists on what the middle-class actually *is*, much less how to measure its vibrancy. What it means to be middle class can certainly vary depending on where you live, your level of education and how much money you make. It's generally accepted that the middle three quintiles (60 percent) of America's income earners are most representative of what we can consider its middle class.

Our concept and image of the middle class has been evolving in the United States since the early 1700s, with the middle class becoming an increasingly influential segment of the American population each passing year. Beginning with the yeoman farmers of the American South, and then evolving to include the factory workers of the industrialized American Northeast, the middle class has ebbed and flowed with social, economic and governmental conditions for about the last 300 years.

However, it was the middle class movement from 1930 onward—sometimes referred to as the *third middle class*—that was by every accepted measure the largest and most inclusive middle-class in American history. It was the granddaddy of all middle classes! And far from being a product of mere circumstance or the "invisible hand" of capitalism, this third and most robust middle class was the culmination of unprecedented (and largely unrepeatable) advances in technology and administration, and very deliberate government action. Simply put, more events took place during this period to raise the prospects of the average working citizen than at any other point preceding it. In other words, this middle class was no accident. It was deliberately and methodically engineered.

In his book *The Myth of the Free Market*, author Mark Anthony Martinez sheds light on the primary ingredients for this historic shift:

> America's third middle class…was made possible by a unique combination of technological, administrative, and government innovations. Specifically, technological advances enabled the "country bumpkin" to become the highly productive and respected American farmer. Technology and administrative advancements urged on by labor law enabled the "greasy mechanic" to become the middle-class assembly line worker. Government policies and other administrative advances turned the American counterpart of the sad and pathetic office worker in Charles Dickens' *A Christmas Carol* into one of the respected accountants and professional bureaucrats seen in government and private offices around the country.

But, as Martinez also points out, the greatest single difference in the middle class of the post-depression era was the historic inception of what his fellow author Michael Lind refers to as the "social wage"—a unique set of social and economic programs administered by government specifically aimed at leveling the economic playing field, protecting the average worker and manufacturing a strong middle class. He suggests that "the social wage has helped level the playing field for a majority of America's middle class by providing better job security, support for unions, improved benefits, and tax incentives." In addition to these policies, the adoption of the G.I. Bill of 1947 provided opportunities for returning servicemen to go to school, start businesses and buy homes—all of which supported increased upward mobility and generally improved standards of living. In turn, this served to close or compress the wealth and income gaps that had always existed but which had also grown to worrisome levels prior to the Great Depression. The distribution of income and wealth was becoming more equitable.

As a result of these and other ongoing social and economic programs, between 1947 and 1979, family wealth and income gaps in America dropped to historic lows, giving rise to an economic period that has been dubbed *The Great Compression*. Real incomes in America grew by a whopping 30 percent between 1952 and 1960, only to be followed up by another 30 percent gain between 1960 and 1968. What's even more crucial to appreciate is that these enormous gains were being evenly distributed across all five income quintiles— not simply congesting among a small number of income earners at the top. The average man and woman were truly better off than they had ever been. Cities abounded with middle-class neighborhoods. Workers enjoyed security and improving wages, which enabled millions to lift themselves from the ranks of the working poor to the promise and safety of the middle class.

The bottom line was that if you were able-bodied, willing to learn and willing to put in an honest day's work, you could not only get a job, you could also get ahead.

The phenomenon wasn't exclusive to the United States either. Indeed Canada, France, Great Britain and many other nations around the world were experiencing their own middle-class renaissance through the same period. In a 1957 speech, Harold Macmillan, Britain's then–prime minister, perhaps said it best: "Let us be frank about it...most of our people have never had it so good. Go around the country, go to the industrial towns, go to the farms and you will see a state of prosperity such as we have never had in my lifetime—nor indeed in the history of this country." Not only was Macmillan absolutely correct, he was actually a little premature, because things were in fact going to get *even better*—not just in Great Britain but in most of the Western world through the 1960s and early 1970s.

It was the perfect storm of favorable conditions. A growing population, rising education levels, positive technological innovation and favorable government taxation and labor policy all conspired to allow average people to educate themselves, buy homes, raise families and secure gainful employment. The result was the largest and most inclusive middle class in history—a group that would ultimately become the most formidable army of consumers the planet had ever seen.

This historic wave of consumers moving up from the working class was a boon to retailers across all categories. New store chains sprang up across North America and existing chains followed their consumers to the suburbs. Retailers fell over themselves to offer new and expanded ranges of products and services to consumers who were in overdrive. Hell, you could buy insurance in a department store!

Life was good for the average American, and that was good for business—at least that's what we believed.

THE BEGINNING OF THE END OF THE MIDDLE

Just as the 1930s and 1940s were the formative decades for the middle class that we know today, many economists point to the 1980s as the starting point of its decline. While very few can deny that this contraction of the middle class is taking place, there is significantly less agreement as to its precise causes and effects. Some argue that government policy became generally adversarial toward labor unions, thus ending the upward trend in wages and benefits seen through the early part of the century. Others suggest that taxation policy tilted in favor of the wealthy, ending a long period of equitable disbursement of earnings and wealth. And still others point to the growing practice of offshoring lower-skilled labor during this period as contributing to higher unemployment and stagnant domestic wages.

Regardless of the exact causes, the statistics make it difficult to dispute that, beginning around 1980, life in the middle got a lot less rosy.

Where the middle class had been advancing by leaps and bounds between 1930 and 1970, the trend had shifted hard into neutral by 1980. In fact, between 1979 and 2005, the after-tax household income of the middle three quintiles (the middle 60 percent) had improved, but only ever so slightly. (See Table 2.1.)

Now, on the face of it, you might feel that this isn't such bad news. After all, people in the middle did make moderately more money—right? The answer, I'm afraid, isn't quite that simple. While it's true that at first glance it seems families were holding their own, there were actually a number of serious underlying problems, many of which economists and politicians are only now beginning to fully comprehend.

First of all, almost 100 percent of the gains in income during that 25-year period are a direct consequence of the addition of a second income earner to the household (usually a female), *not* as a result of a progressive rise in wages,

Table 2.1   Increase in Household Income 1979–2005.

Second Quintile		Middle Quintile		Fourth Quintile	
$4,800	15.8%	$8,700	21.0%	$16,000	29.5%

Source: U.S. Congressional Budget Office

All figures in 2005 constant dollars.

as was the case through the previous five decades. In fact, between 1969 and 2009 the median wage for fully employed men between 30 and 50 years of age actually dropped by a shocking 27 percent, when adjusted for inflation, according to analysis by MIT professor Michael Greenstone. This meant that additional income was coming into households, but—and this is important—for one reason and one reason only: more people were working (and working harder) than ever before.

Secondly, despite these marginal gains in total household income, the average two-income family of 2005 actually had less money left over once they paid their bills, compared to the average one-income family of the 1970s. The problem, you see, was that fixed expenses—the non-negotiable stuff—increased exponentially over the same 25-year span. (See Table 2.2.)

This doesn't even take into account astronomical increases in college and university tuition fees for families that wished to send a child (or two) to school. For many Americans, the prospect of a college education had moved beyond their financial grasp—without borrowing to fund it, that is.

So, while the two-income family was bringing in more dollars in an absolute sense, these gains were being quickly vaporized by enormous increases in fixed living expenses.

There were also new expenses—*lots* of them. Smartphones, wireless plans, high-speed Internet access, computers and, of course, child care. Things that weren't even considerations

Table 2.2   Average Inflation Adjusted Percentage Increase in Fixed Expenses (1979–2005).

Mortgage Payments	76%
Health Insurance	74%
Automobiles	52%
Child Care	100%
Tax Rate (for a two-income family)	25%

Source: U.S. Bureau of Labor Statistics

for families in 1979 had, by the early 2000s, become basic necessities.

It wasn't as though all this was happening overnight. Long before the global financial crisis of 2008, Harvard Law School professor and senator-elect (as of the writing of this book) Elizabeth Warren had been appealing for economists and politicians to take a serious look at what she foresaw as the impending collapse of the middle class. In a 2006 paper on the subject, entitled "The Middle Class on the Precipice: Rising Financial Risks for American Families," Warren described the dilemma that modern, two-income families faced. She wrote that:

> By 2004, the family budget looks very different. As noted earlier, although a man is making nearly $800 less than his counterpart a generation ago, his wife's paycheck brings the family to a combined income that is $73,770—a 75 percent increase. But higher expenses have more than eroded that apparent financial advantage. Their annual mortgage payments are more than $10,500. If they have a child in elementary school who goes to daycare after school and in the summers, the family will spend $5,660. If their second child is a pre-schooler, the cost is even higher—$6,920 a year. With both people in the work-force, the family spends more than $8,000 a year on its two vehicles. Health insurance costs the family $1,970, and taxes now take 30 percent of its money. The bottom line: today's median-earning, median-spending middle-class family sends two people into the workforce, but at the end of the day, they have about $1,500 less for discretionary spending than their one-income counterparts of a generation ago.[1]

 Scan this to watch Elizabeth Warren deliver a brilliant 2007 keynote in which she describes what she foresaw as the coming collapse of the middle class.

So dual-income families were working longer and harder only to end up further behind than their single-income counterparts of 25 years earlier. And if this wasn't enough, another new and potentially catastrophic gamble that families faced was that their lifestyle was now dependent on both heads of the family being fully employed. The family's livelihood hinged on two paychecks, not one. This meant that if one party fell ill, got laid off or was fired, there was no fallback, no plan B. In any such circumstance, it's likely that the family would not be able to meet their obligations—which, in a world with diminishing job security, increased offshoring of employment and automation of routine work, was a real and legitimate concern. Gone were the days when the stay-at-home spouse could simply take a part-time job to help out when the family hit a rough patch. It now took everyone working just to pay the bills.

By 2005, the middle class, which had long been the lubricant of the entire consumer economy, was beginning to seize up under the strain of stagnant wages and escalating living expenses. Where the one-income family of the 1970s was able to maintain their lifestyle while saving up to 11 cents on every dollar coming into the house, their 2005 counterparts were spending more money each year than they earned. For an alarming percentage of households, debt was replacing income as an essential means of staying afloat. Credit card balances alone rose to over $900 billion by 2007, and nearly a quarter of Americans had home-equity lines of credit totaling more than a trillion dollars, up from one billion, only 25 years earlier—an increase of more than 1,000 percent!

For millions of families this meant that while they believed they were working their way toward the American dream, they were actually rapidly running farther and farther away from it.

SHOW ME THE MONEY!

Now, you might be wondering, how can it be that while the U.S. economy was growing in leaps and bounds from 1980 to 2005, the middle class was actually contracting? It certainly does seem a little counterintuitive that the economy could be doing so tremendously well but the average American family so poorly. Any logical person would be prompted to ask: If all this money didn't land in the middle, where *did* it go?

It's a fact that between 1980 and 2005, the U.S. economy doubled in size. Corporations were posting record profits, the number of Americans declaring over a million dollars in income on their tax returns grew eightfold between 1982 and 1987 and the Dow index rose from 776.92 in 1982 to 2722.42 in 1987.[2] The economy was on fire!

The spoils of all this growth, however, were not at all evenly distributed. In fact, while wages for middle-income earners remained flat and even lost ground, incomes for the top 20 percent of households rose by approximately 79 percent.[3] And as far as growth in the stock market was concerned, more than two-thirds of Americans held no stock whatsoever, so any gains in the stock market were completely inconsequential to the average American. No longer were the country's economic gains finding their way into the hands of the average middle-class family—just the contrary. During the same period, the percentage of families occupying the middle class dropped, and the number of middle-class neighborhoods in American cities plummeted.

Some argue that while the ranks of the middle class may indeed have been depleting over the last 30 years, this wasn't purely a matter of families falling into the ranks of the poor. Instead, they claim, it's as much a result of families moving *up the ladder* into the ranks of the wealthy. While this may be true in a minority of cases, there's not a shred of evidence to support this claim's validity on a wide scale. What is verifiable, however, is that many of the same corporations posting record earnings during the 1980s and 1990s were able to do so by eliminating middle-skilled jobs. Factories closed across the country, wiping out millions of blue-collar positions. With few other options, many of these displaced middle-skilled workers had little choice but to take lower-paying service positions—often at a fraction of their previous earnings levels. There were no rungs on the ladder left for them to climb.

Meanwhile, those in high income brackets were making fortunes. In his book *The Great Divergence*, author Timothy Noah notes that in 1979 the incomes in the top 20 percent were, on average, eight times those of the bottom 20 percent.[4] By 2005, however, the spread had become 14 times that of the bottom 20 percent. What had been a robust and growing middle class was now being hollowed out as incomes and wealth sharply polarized. The division between rich and poor was widening to become a chasm.

The middle class was being systematically and steadily gutted.

THE IMPERFECT STORM

So, just as the post-Depression and postwar eras spawned the perfect combination of circumstances to bolster the middle class, the 1980s, 1990s and early 2000s brought an equally potent formula for its dismantlement. Economists and politicians fiercely debate what's specifically to blame for the contraction of the middle, and while it's not my intention here to delve deep into each of the potential culprits, it's important that we at least touch on some of the primary ones.

The Weakening of Labor Unions: On August 5, 1981, in response to an illegal strike by the Professional Air Traffic Controllers Organization (PATCO), newly inaugurated President Ronald Reagan took action by firing over 11,000 members of the union and banning them from civil service for life. This unprecedented move was regarded by many as a watershed moment that set into motion the systematic weakening of the labor movement, which, to this day, has never fully regained its stature or bargaining power.

Lagging Minimum Wage: Beginning in 2007, Washington began to make small upward adjustments to federal minimum wage, which stood at $5.15 for the previous 10 years.

The government took it first to $5.85, then to $6.55 in 2008 and finally to $7.25 in 2009, where it remains today. It's hard to dispute the significance of the increase on a percentage basis, and yet many point out that this figure still woefully lags 30 years of cumulative inflation and should, in fact, be somewhere well above $10.00.

Shift to the Knowledge Economy: Where the postwar era saw the addition of millions of low- and middle-skilled jobs, the 1980s ushered in the era of the knowledge worker. Increasingly, the financial benefits of economic growth were concentrated among fewer and more highly trained workers, whose families could fund their increasingly expensive higher educations. While some of the lower-skilled workers who were displaced in the transition may have been able to upgrade their knowledge and actually move into skilled positions, they were the minority. Many simply slid down the economic ladder. The fallout of the winding down of North America's industrial economy continues today, as it increasingly cedes to the digital era.

Globalization/Offshoring: The opening and ramping up of trade with a host of developing countries eroded the need for, and advantage of, domestic manufacturing. Sourcing products and services from places like China, Indonesia and India became table stakes for many businesses struggling to compete with companies like Walmart who, according to the Economic Policy Institute, was single-handedly responsible for 11 percent of the growth in the U.S. trade deficit with China between 2001 and 2006, as imports rose from $9 billion to $27 billion over that six-year period. Owing to this and other pressures, companies across categories began looking for offshore alternatives. Subsequently, over 40,000 American factories closed, displacing millions of blue-collar workers and their middle managers. Ironically, the retailer that prided itself on helping the average American family save money and "live better" is the same company that, at least in part, contributed directly to the hardship of the very middle class it served.

Government Policy: Throughout the 1980s, 1990s and 2000s, the political bent of Washington took a noticeable turn away from the individuals and families in the middle and moved decidedly more in favor of corporate America and individuals at the upper reaches of the income pyramid. Taxation and social welfare policies that had for decades contributed to the growth of the middle class were gradually cut back and/ or dismantled completely. In fact, changes to taxation policy through the 1980s actually raised the effective tax rate by 16.6 percent for low-income Americans while cutting it by 14.4 percent for the wealthiest.

My objective in telling you all this is not to pass judgment or perform a morality play about the social merits of the middle class—you're entitled to follow your own political and social compass on that. My real interest lies only in helping you to realize that if you still believe that your business is serving a middle class that looks anything like the middle class of the 1970s, you're deluding yourself.

How the disappearing middle happened, when it happened and who was ultimately responsible can and will continue to be debated. What matters is the undeniable reality that this thing we call the middle class is shrinking and rapidly ceasing to be a primary driver of retail consumption on this continent.

Today, the top 5 percent of income earners in the United States is responsible for an astonishing 37 percent of all consumer outlays. To comprehend the magnitude of this, consider that the bottom 80 percent of income earners is responsible for only 39 percent (a mere 2 percent more).

What makes this new market more difficult for retailers to navigate is that consumer preferences and behaviors can't be neatly categorized by economic strata the way they once could. The discount shopper at 10 a.m. might very well be breathing the rarified air at a Mercedes dealership later that day. Gross family income has become a dramatically less reliable determinant of specific brand and product propensity as consmers migrate between the extremes of value. In a world with a disappearing middle, that sense of value is being completely redefined. Consumers, who are infinitely more thoughtful in how they spend, are now consistently shunning average, mid-market retail propositions in favor of brands, products and services with clearer, more defined value equations. They're aggressively saving money on things that don't matter to them, in order to spend lavishly on the things that do. Everything in the middle is simply invisible.

STUCK IN THE MIDDLE WITH YOU

When I began my career as a retail marketer in the early 1990s, pricing just about any product or service was a cinch as long as you followed one simple formula. The "good, better, best" pricing convention that most retail marketers had used for the last 60 years was a surefire model for pricing just about anything from TVs to tennis rackets. Anywhere you shopped, you would have likely seen this simple three-tier pricing model in action. It was ironclad!

"Good" was the entry-level line in a category. It was engineered, as one might guess, to be *just good enough* so as to be passable from a quality standpoint, but not *so good* as to deliver outstanding performance. The "good" line was the bait, so to speak, that you used to draw customers to the threshold of your store. Once you lured them in, you could then try to convert them to a higher-priced line of product. Consequently, as a marketer, you had to keep a wary eye on competitors to ensure that you weren't being undercut on these important entry-level lines. From the retailer's standpoint, there was generally very little profit in selling the "good" line of product, but, again, its purpose wasn't profit—it was a pawn used to support the perception of your chain as competitively positioned in the market.

At the other end of the spectrum was the "best" line of product. This was far and away the highest price point in a given category, and because volume in these lines typically trailed the lower-priced alternatives, they often made up for it with very high profit percentages. Products in this tier weren't always distinctly different or unique from other lines. In fact, in some cases, they were just slight reworks or even repackaged versions of other lines. Regardless, this was the product that every sales person on the store floor was instructed and perhaps incentivized to upsell to customers—regardless of whether they needed that level of quality or not. For the customer to whom brand and status mattered most, it was the obvious choice. And when you wanted some real excitement, you needed only to run a discount on your "best" line and consumers would literally line up for it.

Finally, smack dab in the middle, there was the "better" or mid-tier line of product. With just the right amount of engineering to be of average quality, the better product occupied the sweet spot from a pricing standpoint. With comfortable price points, it was an easy upsell from the "good" line, and a simple step down from the "best" line. Consequently, the midline was usually king of the category. Not only did it drive the majority of unit sales, it was also the profit cow, contributing the majority of gross profit dollars to the company's bottom line. It was the product that the company depended on to pay the bills.

There are a few reasons why this model worked so well. First of all, three choices are manageable from an analytical perspective—a choice of three doesn't confuse our brains the way more choices would. Second, the system allays two of the shopper's greatest fears: spending too little and getting *crap*, or spending too much and getting ripped off. But there's another overarching reason why good, better, best worked. Most customers felt that they *belonged* to the middle. They felt that their lifestyles, their economic states and therefore their product needs were no better or worse than average. The average choice was the most popular choice because most people ate, played, stayed, wore, drove, and wanted to be in the middle. The middle was what they aspired to. The middle was where they lived!

The mid-tier used to be where every brand wanted to play. Now, it's competitive purgatory.

Which leads me back to Sears. If truth be told, there was never anything particularly spectacular about the Sears experience. And that's precisely why it worked so well. Sears was simply a mid-market store, selling mid-tier products to the ever-growing ranks of the middle class that was eager for the trappings of the middle-income lifestyle. The goods were neither expensive nor cheap, neither luxurious nor bargain basement. Sears stores, products and services were simply average—just like their customers. Which is precisely why Sears doesn't work anymore and hasn't for decades. It's average.

But to harp on Sears isn't really fair. It just happens to be a highly visible case study of a brand that didn't respond to key changes in society. However, if you take a look around, I can assure you that on every street corner there are companies that find themselves in exactly the same position—stuck in the middle. Your company may even be one of them, fighting over a customer base that simply doesn't exist anymore, doing what you did in 1979 and wondering why it's no longer working.

The hard truth is that the big, fat middle is decaying—and has been for more than 30 years. More people are leaving the middle class each year than are joining it. A small percentage of the wealthy are accounting for greater and greater proportions of consumer outlays, and the rest of us are barely matching that small, elite percentage's spending power. In this landscape, being "good" just won't cut it anymore. My parents were satisfied to settle for *average*—today's consumer will not.

So if you're still shooting for the middle, I'm afraid you'll miss every time, because the middle, as we knew it, is gone for good.

3

Rest in Peace, Joe Average

AT A RECENT KEYNOTE PRESENTATION, I stood in front of a hundred or so marketers who represented brands that were sponsors in a major North American loyalty program. The audience was a very cool cross section of the retail marketplace, comprised of categories from apparel and hardware to travel, grocery and entertainment—to name only a few. At one point in the presentation I displayed an image of a very stereotypical-looking family—a white couple in their early to mid-40s with two clean-cut, straight-toothed children. The family was well groomed and well clothed, definitely middle to upper-middle income. The only additional stereotype missing was the golden retriever.

Out of interest, I asked by a show of hands how many marketers in the room believed that this family was their target consumer—the very consumer they see in their mind's eye when they go to work each morning. I wasn't surprised with the large show of hands—about 80 percent of the audience. I tested the room a little further, saying, "Now keep your hand raised if you foresee this family continuing to represent your target consumer group five to ten years from now." Few in the room dropped their hands.

Not surprisingly, regardless of what products or services this audience of marketers sold, they were pursuing the same demographic target. Almost unanimously they characterized the focus of their pursuit as the "average" or "typical" North American family—the kind you see portrayed in so many marketing pieces. And perhaps most importantly, most felt that this "typical" family would continue to be a bull's-eye for their brand well into the foreseeable future.

All of this would have been perfectly fine, save for one major kink: this typical family *no longer exists*.

"I am intimidated by the fear of being average."

— *Taylor Swift*

"STINCHCOMBED"

In the mid-1960s, sociologist Arthur L. Stinchcombe developed a hypothesis with respect to the manner in which organizations originate and evolve. Observing that organizations that formed at different times often have different structures and develop quite differently, Stinchcombe theorized that "organizations which are founded at a particular time must construct their social systems with the social resources available."[1] More simply put, organizations are founded on and guided according to the social, economic, political and technological realities of their time. This set of circumstances becomes their founding context—it's who they are. Stinchcombe called this the theory of "organizational imprinting." I call it a company's DNA.

If all this strikes you as being pretty obvious, wait—because there's more. Beyond simply being foundational, Stinchcombe believed that these founding perspectives on the world could actually persist for decades or even centuries, impeding the organization's ability to adapt to change—even when failure to do so could result in obliteration. In other words, the lens through which an organization views the world can be so badly obscured by its founding context that the organization becomes utterly unable (and sometimes just unwilling) to change. Consequently, the organization becomes irrelevant, withers and dies.

Today's business landscape is littered with organizations that got "Stinchcombed"(they saw the world through the lens of a different time, and suffered as a result). Best Buy, founded in a world without the Internet, struggles today to find relevance now that online retail is ubiquitous and product selection has been redefined. Blockbuster video was born during a time without streaming digital content, and became the victim of wholly web-based Netflix. Research In Motion—at one time, the world's most successful maker of smartphones continued to see the market as it was in 2003: a place where smartphones were almost purely a business tool. By the time it realized otherwise, Apple and others had already penetrated the consumer market so deeply that it couldn't catch up. Even Facebook, which was founded on the cusp of the social networking movement, is now struggling to find its place in an increasingly mobile-oriented world. No one, it seems, is immune to the deadly infection of organizational imprinting.

So, had Arthur Stinchcombe been in the room that day as a majority of marketers pointed to this "average family" as their core target, I suspect he would have worn a knowing smile. Indeed, the reason so many in the room believed that their customer was white, middle class and married with children is because, when most of their companies were founded, *they were*!

ASPIRING TO BE AVERAGE

In 1962, when Sam Walton and so many others began revving their respective retail engines, not only were families raising what would come to be known as the baby boom generation, but the average American also had access to stable employment and growing disposable income. And if that wasn't enough to make cash registers hum in anticipation, most Americans shared the same general needs, tastes and preferences when shopping. Sure, there may have been differences between a family in New York and one in Chicago or San Francisco, but compared to today, these differences were mere nuances. For the most part, norms regarding family composition, marital status, child rearing and gender roles were consistent across much of the continent.

Remember, most people *aspired to be average* and to have the material things and quality of life that other families had. So whether your name was De Luca, Dietrich or Davidowitz, you, like everyone else, were keeping up with the Joneses and wanted exactly what they had. No more, no less. Yes, the holy trinity of retail was complete. More people, with more money and most wanting exactly the same things! Halle-freakin-lujah!

It was at this exact, incredible and never-to-be-repeated point in history that the formula for success that Walmart and other major retailers used to grow first became feasible. It was an ironclad system, and it went like this:

Step 1: Broadly project consumer product needs and preferences across each product category in as narrow a range of goods as possible.

Step 2: Buy high enough volumes in that narrow range of items to garner significant purchasing power and leverage over vendors.

Step 3: Sell those goods out over a reasonable period using mass media and/or aggressive pricing strategies while demanding that vendors swap out slow-moving stock before introducing new lines.

If you could pull off all three steps while managing back-end costs and efficiencies, you could make a fortune. You didn't have to have beautifully appointed stores and you didn't have to train staff to provide anything but mediocre service. You just needed to follow the three steps and do it as efficiently as possible. And it all worked perfectly because consumers had almost no other choice but to wait for brands and retailers to *tell them* what they should want. There was no digital pipeline of trends that consumers could tap into—no pixilated window on the world. Hell, merely uttering the word "Google" in 1962 might have landed you in a psych ward.

So, to Stinchcombe's point, with so many of the companies we currently work for having their genesis in this particularly fertile period of the early to mid-1960s, the tendency in those organizations to this day is to regard the world through the psychedelic glasses of that founding era. They still believe now what was true then: that there is indeed an average, typical and very targetable family with highly predictable tastes and preferences that can be instructed by retailers on what they ought to want and aspire to.

This, of course, is no longer the case, and nothing could have driven the point home more clearly than the results of the 2010 U.S. census. Page after page abruptly illustrated how the unique social and economic conditions that forged our image of the "average" consumer were coming unglued, giving rise to new and unique individuals and households who are anything but typical.

A recent PricewaterhouseCoopers report may have put it best, saying that marketers would be well advised to stop thinking in terms of "families," and rather in terms of "households."[2]

The entire concept of "family" is shifting and evolving more rapidly today than at any point in recent history. The reasons are many: economic pressures, evolving societal mores, emerging ethno-cultural norms and even technology.

Together, these forces are bringing to a close the era of the traditional nuclear family, as retailers have known (and loved) it. However, in its wake is a crosscurrent of new markets and tremendous opportunities.

So, with all that said, let's take ourselves to a cruising altitude of 50,000 feet for a look at how this concept of the average family is being and will continue to be forever changed.

Marriage

If you were to accept the ads you saw on television and in magazines as even a loose reflection of reality, you'd believe that most of America was blissfully married. Ad after ad shows what appear to be married couples smooching, walking on the beach and making purchasing decisions about everything from ShamWows to mutual funds. In fact, nothing could be further from the truth. To put it bluntly, marriage is out of fashion.

Both Americans and Canadians are marrying in lower numbers than ever before. The reasons are many and mixed: greater social acceptance of single parenthood, same-sex unions, common-law relationships and extraordinary divorce rates are all partially responsible. The sketchy economic landscape and bottomless real estate market are also prompting many to postpone marriage.

According to the Pew Research Center, almost 50 percent of American adults are single—a record percentage. In 1960, only 28 percent of the adult population was single. In addition, the Pew Research Center reports that "the median age at first marriage has never been higher for brides (26.5 years) and grooms (28.7)." Globally, more than 200 million people worldwide are *settling down* as singles—a 33-percent increase between 1996 and 2006.[3]

It's estimated that at the current rate of decline, the number of married individuals will drop to below half of people above 18 years old within a few short years.

But does being single mean *living alone*? Of the 96 million people in the United States who claimed to be single in 2010,

61 percent had never uttered the words "I do." And 31 million of them lived completely alone, accounting for a whopping 27 percent of American households—a 10-percent increase since 1970.

Yet, despite this glaring reality, we still live in a world where being single is treated as the exception and is very often penalized. Consider that only a small percentage of food in the local grocery store is sold in a single-serving quantity, and what *is* there is priced at a steep premium. Single travelers are still clobbered with an additional charge for being single. Insurance rates are often higher for singles. And, to top it all off, single people typically pay higher taxes, while families with children reap tax incentives.

We've designed the entire consumer world for (and continue to cater to) what is now a growing *minority* of consumers. In essence, we punish people for choosing to live on their own. It's like a tax on solitude.

One can only imagine the opportunity that awaits retailers who figure out how to serve the single market without gouging them—to celebrate singledom instead of applying a surtax to it!

Multigenerational Households

Kids are living at home longer—much longer. In fact, the proportion of adult children living with their parents today is higher than at any time since the 1950s. It seems beyond coincidence that the percentage of multigenerational households follows almost perfectly the post-1980 stagnation of middle incomes in America. The rising costs of home ownership, coupled with static middle incomes and a flagging employment market, have made the adolescent launch from the nest more challenging than at any time in the last 60 years.

There's a danger, however, in painting the circumstances of all multigenerational households with the same economic brush. In upper-income families, for example, adult children may live at home while upgrading their postsecondary education in order to prepare them for higher-skilled and higher-paying employment—arguably a good thing. In contrast, working-class parents may need an adult child to remain at home to help pay the rent and stay afloat financially—arguably a bad thing and an impediment to the child. In other cases, it's *culture* and not *economics* that is the impetus for the multigenerational household. Extended family living arrangements are simply more commonplace (and even an expectation) in many Hispanic and Asian cultures. It is not considered unusual to find young families moving in with their parents. So, it's also no coincidence that multigenerational influence has grown with increased Hispanic and Asian immigration.

Regardless of the catalysts, what is certain is that a growing number of households contain multiple consumers and multiple influencers, all of whom have unique needs. This presents new issues for marketers. Where brands and retailers could once make relatively accurate assumptions about a household and its occupants based on the age, occupation and income of the head of household, that's simply not as true when more and more homes contain up to three consumer segments under one roof.

Child Rearing

More Americans are choosing to own dogs than have children. Despite an overall population growth since 1990 of almost 1 percent per annum, the number of children in the country has remained flat, leading to a 2.5-percent reduction in households with children. Quite simply, fewer children are being born, and women, on average, are waiting longer to have them.

Children make up about 24 percent of the U.S. population, down from 26 percent in 1990. Experts maintain that percentage could dip to 23 percent by 2050.[4] Contrast this with the fact that in 1900, kids made up 40 percent of the population, and you can see just how dramatic the drop-off has been. However, these statistics pale in comparison when you consider the demographics of other countries around the world.

For example, an astounding 50 percent of the population of Uganda is under 15. *15!* So tell me, all other things being equal, if you sell kids' shoes, would you rather set up shop in the United States or Uganda?

Not only does this growing childlessness trend in the West and elsewhere presage long-term issues with respect to supporting social programs for an aging population, it makes a marketer's job a lot harder. Certain events in a consumer's life, like marriage, the birth of children and even death, act as very reliable milestones that allow marketers to pinpoint, project and anticipate other major purchases—family cars, life insurance, larger homes, trips to Disney World and, yes, even coffins. These life markers also give marketers easy ways to interrupt consumers with offers. I recall receiving a gift basket at the hospital after the arrival of our baby daughter that was sponsored by major consumer brands. Little did my wife and I know at the time that that single basket of baby products would be the catalyst for decades of direct marketing from companies using the marker of our daughter's birth to anticipate our potential product and service needs.

With fewer children being born, the task of identifying eligible consumers and following them through their lives becomes more complex, requiring new and more sophisticated tools and a very different marketing approach in general.

Single-Parent Families

If I told you that 29 percent of your customers prefer paper bags to plastic, chances are you'd give serious consideration to getting in some paper bags, pronto! Likewise, if I could prove that 40 percent of your customers liked to shop late on Wednesday nights, I bet you'd be open on Wednesday nights.

Yet, there are plenty of equally compelling statistics that seem to be falling on deaf retail ears. For example:

- Today, 29 percent of American households with children are headed by a single parent.

And if that doesn't blow your mind...

- Forty percent of children in America are born to single women—a sixfold increase since 1960[5]—and this while teen pregnancy has been declining!

And if you think it's strictly a matter of ethnic background...

- While African Americans have the highest absolute percentage of single-parent births, Hispanics and whites have seen the highest *increase* in percentage of single-parent births.

And if you think this is all about unwed mothers...

- Males are the fastest growing category of single parents.[6]

And if you think most of these single parents require government financial assistance...

- Seventy-nine percent of single moms and 92 percent of single dads are gainfully employed, with the vast majority receiving nothing in the way of government assistance.

The question is, which retailers among us are reaching out to this growing community to show an understanding of their daily challenges? Who's stepping up to create a shopping experience conducive to the unique lifestyle, needs and challenges of the single parent? Anybody?

One of my clients is in the airline industry. To assist with a project, I undertook some informal research with audiences around North America. I asked how many people had taken a long flight with a young child and with no other adult along. Inevitably, there were a few people in each audience who had taken a flight with a child only. I then asked how many of them, while on that trip, felt (even for a minute) as though the airline experience had been designed for them and their situation. Surprisingly, out of hundreds who had flown with a child, *not one* of them felt that their needs had been considered or that the carrier had tried to make their trip easier. Most rated the experience somewhere between a root canal and hives.

It seems that most organizations are either knowingly or unknowingly overlooking single moms and dads as a viable and distinct segment. This is sadly ironic considering that single parents may actually be more receptive to brand messaging than their two-parent counterparts. One recent study out of the UK suggested that brands actually have a greater chance and ability to connect and resonate emotionally with single parents than with married consumers with children.[7] It points to the single parent's greater potential core need for connection, belonging and escapism.

Gender

Retailers have long recognized the influence that women have over how family income is spent. It's been estimated that up to 80 percent of every dollar spent is directly influenced by the female of the household. Consequently, much of what we see and experience in retail stores was engineered with the female shopper in every marketer's mind's eye.

Today, however, things are different and the stakes are even higher. Women are no longer simply influencing how the dollars are being spent; to a growing extent, they are the ones controlling how the dollars are being *earned*.

Simply put, women are doing better than men—if not in absolute dollars, at least in terms of percentage gains. Their participation in the labor force continues to grow and is expected to reach a majority by 2018.[8] Women also account for 51 percent of managerial positions in the United States, up from a mere 26 percent in 1980. And beyond simply working more and in greater numbers, women are also being paid more as well. In fact, single, childless women make an average of 8 percent more than their male counterparts. Not too shabby.

Scan this to see just how far women have come in a mere 50 years!

Men, on the other hand, are living in their parents' basements longer.

To be fair to my brethren, there is no question that at least some of this trend is attributable to the disproportionate fallout that many men suffered during the recession. Indeed, up to 80 percent of the job losses suffered in the recession have been jobs held by men, leading some to call it a *he-cession*.

Having said that, it's also critical to understand that the trend toward female empowerment began prior to the recession and, in fact, has its roots in education and socialization— set in motion long before women arrived in the workplace in numbers.

Women are the majority of college graduates, representing about 57 percent of enrollments at American colleges since at least 2000, according to the American Council on Education. The reasons for this run the gamut from women having higher grades on average to men dropping out of school more frequently. Bottom line: women are more frequently receiving better educations, and this is leading to employability and first-time home ownership rates that are higher than those of their male counterparts.

One also can't overlook the fact that much of the money being poured into the economy from government is hitting sectors such as heath care, education and social services, which have traditionally been female-dominated fields.

And, while it's estimated that 80 percent of the jobs created since the recession have been filled by men, there is ample evidence to suggest that men have traded down to jobs at lower wages and skill requirements. As we've seen all too often, workers have had to trade good-paying factory jobs, out of sheer necessity, for lower-paying service jobs.

Beyond the current economic turmoil, however, some see this issue of gender roles as a more fundamental societal evolution and one that will change business forever. Marketing futurist Faith Popcorn sees it as part of a much broader trend that she calls "EnGen"—the end of the gender wars, and the feminization of society as a whole. Popcorn sees the rise of a new kind of workplace where more traditionally feminine qualities such as empathy, listening and understanding begin to displace balls, brawn and brazenness as the means by which things get done in corporations.

She further claims (and I agree with her completely) that what all of this is really leading to is the end of "one-dimensional identities" based on gender. On a growing basis, men and women will share, trade and interchange roles and responsibilities in their lives very fluidly and without concern for gender stereotypes. Traditional male and female domains, particularly with respect to consumerism, will fall by the wayside.

This may be petrifying for retailers who have thrived in a *pink and blue world* where he bought the beer and she shopped for baby. That was straightforward! This growing gender neutrality, however, while opening up new opportunities, requires a different marketing and retailing approach. But let's be clear: what this does not mean is simply merchandising the beer, razors and *Playboy* magazines together in a "man aisle," as some retailers have begun doing. This is just lazy marketing that I liken to putting pink handles on power tools to sell to women. It pays lip service to something much more momentous and deserving of genuine understanding.

The reality is that over 30 percent of men report being the primary household grocery shopper—up from 14 percent in 1985. In addition, men are out-shopping women when it comes to online luxury goods. There is also evidence that suggests that young men have a decidedly more positive perception of shopping than older men, because their shopping tendencies and category interests more closely resemble those of women. Some identify men who enjoy shopping with the almost pejorative "metrosexual" label, which I think is wrong. Just as women have discovered newfound freedom to express themselves in the workplace, men are becoming comfortable as shoppers.

Smart retailers will look beyond the "man aisle" and other patronizing gestures and focus instead on something far more important: making the shopping experience better for all customers, regardless of gender.

Aging

Consumers in the United States, Canada and much of the developed world are aging. No surprise there. What *is* surprising, however, is just how few companies have a handle on how to adapt to it. Very few of the major brands and chains that I meet with have any defined path laid out for how to treat the issue of aging among their customers. Most are continuing to do exactly the same things they've always done, while hoping a strategy of some sort will present itself.

Sure, we're seeing some shrinking of store footprints and tightening of product selections, but much of this is the retailer's response to tough economic times, not a sincere desire to provide a better shopping experience for aging consumers. The truth is that there are few case studies that speak to concrete examples of retail adaptation to the aging consumer market.

In the industry's defense, however, this is all very unfamiliar ground. Consider that as late as 1900, the average life expectancy in the United States was a mere 47 years. Today it's 78 in the United States and 81 in Canada! Incredibly, in just a little over a century, we've begun living almost twice as long! So, to be fair, anyone who even claims to have this *aging consumer thing* all sorted out is deluding himself. We've never been here before. This came fast and it's not letting up.

By 2029, all baby boomers (those born between 1946 and 1964) will be over the age of 65, and one in four people in the country will be a senior citizen. By 2016, more seniors than children will make up the Canadian populace. By 2025, the same will be true of one-third of all U.S. states. And, in one short year, *all* baby boomers will be over the age of 50—the twilight where, according to the Bureau of Labor Statistics, consumer spending typically begins to decline precipitously. At 50, we simply need less stuff than we do in our prime replacement spending years.

This statistical reality has in no small part been a huge contributing factor in our stubbornly suppressed economic recovery. Whatever economic stability has been gained post 2008 is being simultaneously undermined by this natural drop-off in 50-plus boomer spending, which broadens to more and more consumers and categories of goods with each passing year.

Despite this natural denouement in spending as we age, most brands, retail chains, shopping venues and indeed entire cities are still betting heavy on boomers to carry the economy. The question, however, is *which* boomers?

There's a dangerous tendency for marketers to lump all baby boomers together regardless of age, when in fact they can be as different as night and day. For example, my sister Wendy was born in 1947. I was born in 1964. On paper, we're both baby boomers, but in just about every other respect— economically, technologically, politically and otherwise— we're different, and with good reason. Very different events shaped our lives. Unique circumstances formed our behaviors and attitudes. To offer Wendy and me an identical marketing pitch would be naive and would very likely fail. So, if your company hasn't already done so, it needs to decide which segment of the boomers it is really trying to reach. The ones who protested Vietnam and listened to Jimi Hendrix, or the ones who followed the Iran hostage crisis and watched MTV? To whom exactly are you talking?

And you really need to get that right, because connecting with the wrong subsegment could present problems. For example, a product that is popular among leading-edge baby boomers may, in fact, have gone the way of pet rocks for trailing-edge boomers. As *Slate* tech columnist Farhad Manjoo points out, this is precisely the fate that befell Microsoft's Hotmail—which had recently been revamped to compete with Gmail. Manjoo wrote: "The problem with Hotmail isn't how it works, it's the service's digital standing. A hotmail.com email address long ago became a mark of naiveté, an address for grandmas and other schemers. Telling people to contact you at Hotmail was an invitation for ridicule—the Internet equivalent of wearing a Kick Me sign."[9] So, the very success that Hotmail had with leading-edge boomers likely contributed to it falling out of fashion with younger boomers.

It's clear that treating baby boomers as one large group, all sharing the same likes, dislikes and needs, is folly. It just won't work. And this doesn't even account for loads of psychographic data that provide even more dimension and nuance to how we characterize these consumers. The state of mind, opinions, attitudes and unique outlooks that various boomers have will subsegment them even further. In other words, all boomers were not born (and will not age) equal!

Perhaps the most pervasive misconception surrounding baby boomers is that most will be retiring with boatloads of money and will be sipping champagne cocktails on a distant beach. In reality, according to a recent poll by the AARP, almost three-quarters of baby boomers polled anticipate the need to delay retirement, and 50 percent fear they may *never* be able to retire.[10] Never! Of those who expect to retire, 65 percent worry that they will not have the means to live comfortably once they stop working.

Again, this condition is not shouldered evenly across all baby boomers. Studies suggest that older boomers are, on average, about 11 percent better prepared for retirement than their younger boomer counterparts.[11] However, it will hardly be the silver-haired tropical spending bonanza that many marketers envisioned pre-2008.

Of particular concern is the extent to which boomers are accumulating debt. At a time when most should be feathering the nest of retirement and burning mortgages, boomers on both sides of the border are actually taking on *more* credit.

In the United States, average overall debt for 55-and-older households more than doubled from 1992 to 2007, topping out at $70,370.[12] And, shockingly, consumers with the highest credit card balances outstanding are in the 65-and-over age range.

Finally, there are the physical constraints that are an inevitable part of aging. Sure, baby boomers may be aging differently than their parents, but they will undoubtedly age nonetheless. That means that if you're hanging your hopes on baby boomer spending, you'd be wise to begin tinkering with elements of the store experience now.

The following are just a few of the things that retailers and manufacturers will need to consider.

Store Layouts	clear, right-sized and easy to shop with intuitive navigation to avoid shopper confusion
Lighting	bright and color-corrected to account for failing vision
Ambient Noise Levels	reduced to account for increased use of hearing aids
Product Weights	heavy items logically placed in the store, and carryout assistance available
Font Sizes	signs, documents and contracts highly legible
Shelf Heights	adjusted to reduce bending and reaching
Lines and Wait Times	have to be reduced or eliminated
Packaging	should be easy to carry, easy to open and include easy-to-decipher instructions
Portions/ Quantities	need to be rethought for lower rates of consumption
Fitting Rooms	must be attended and well serviced to make trying things on easy
Policies	clear, straightforward and intelligible to avoid confusion and conflict
Service Levels	leverage technology or manpower to provide remarkable service

Transportation and Delivery Services	need to be rethought to take into account a decrease in the number of baby boomer drivers; creative solutions needed to get customers to the store and products to the customer
Ancillary Service Offerings	as fewer products are required, consider what new services might be valuable or useful for customers
Web and Mobile Applications	must be clean, utilitarian and quick

What you may have noticed is that just about every consideration required to make the store more inviting to aging consumers would, in fact, contribute to a better shopping experience for *all consumers*, regardless of their age. In other words, it may take 100 million aging boomers to instigate retail upgrades that should have happened a long time ago!

All in all, no other generation in the history of the world has had such a profound social and economic impact as the post–World War II baby boom. As they adapt to old age, retail will need to adapt with them.

The days of pandering to seniors with a 10-percent discount on Wednesdays are over. The entire retail experience has to be revamped.

Millennials

Millennials, or Generation Y, as they're often called, have become almost mythical creatures in marketing circles, legendary for their prolific spending, brand awareness and ability to "make it rain dead presidents" for retailers with their three- and four-digit allowances! They are frequently referred to as digital natives—screen junkies who are always connected and comfortable in any buying channel. They are viewed by some marketers as big on brands but low on loyalty, switching one product or retailer for another with frequency more commonly afforded to dirty socks. They are seen basically as a huge tribe of racially diverse, attention-depleted, Red Bull–guzzling shopping freaks! This, my friends, is the Millennial Generation as the marketing community has portrayed them.

But as with all consumer segmentation, the challenge is separating the genuine from the generalized, the fact from the fiction.

First, let's get to the truth. It is true that Millennials are not afraid of technology, and many are almost always connected to their friends via social networks. Forty percent report visiting Facebook more than 10 times per day. However, this should not be taken to mean that they are the predominant users of *all* technology platforms. They aren't. But they are fearless in their ability to navigate new platforms, networks and devices. They use technology quite intuitively.

As table 3.1 suggests, they are also very racially diverse — far more so than their parents or grandparents. Almost one in two Americans under the age of 15 is a visible minority.

It's not unusual to hear marketers bemoaning Gen Y for what they see as a lack of loyalty. The generation has garnered a reputation for loving and then leaving brands almost as quickly. It's unfair though to say that Millennials are not loyal. They simply define loyalty very differently

Table 3.1   *Percentage of Population By Age and Race.*[13]

	Age						
	<15	15–24	25–34	35–44	45–54	55–64	65–74
Asian American	6	6	6	6	5	4	4
African American	14	14	14	14	12	11	9
Hispanic	22	20	17	16	13	10	8
White	57	59	62	63	· 68	74	79
Other*	1	1	1	1	2	1	0

*"Other" race is not shown on census form.

than older consumers. One study suggested that the average Millennial mom feels that sticking with a brand for six to twelve months *is* being loyal! So, what's prompting such short windows of loyalty? One can't help but think that part of this is merely a result of the sheer amount of choice available to Millennials that was *not* available to their parents at the same age. When I was a kid, if you wanted jeans you could buy Levi's or Lee and maybe a few other brands. Today, there are hundreds of brands of jeans. If you wanted a soft drink in 1972, you had a choice of brands that could fill a small cooler. Today, The Coca-Cola Company alone has a portfolio of over 3,500 beverages worldwide! How could *anyone* remain loyal over the long term in a world with so much choice? And it's not just the choice that's key, it's also the unprecedented access that young people have to that choice that's the game changer. Teens aren't relying on some fashion buyer at a department store to tell them what's cool — they're discovering it themselves. They're not relying on a marketer to tell them what to drink — they're discovering new beverages themselves. They don't simply respond to trends — they set them.

Finally, it is absolutely true that Millennials spent disproportionately more money on consumer goods, even adjusting for inflation, than their parents did at the same age. It is also true that their tastes included very upscale brands. The question is, how will these behaviors shift in a post-recession world? How much of what we perceived to be at the root of Generation Y's behavior was predicated on wild and wacky pre-2008 economics (an era that every retailer should file under "never again")?

Some point to historic unemployment, the burden of student loans and the rising cost of living as stakes through the heart of the Millennials' shopping prowess. And there's something to be said for this position. After all, it has been well documented that young people who begin their working lives during troubled economic times can carry a burden of much-lower-than-average income for years — even decades.

When this is coupled with the astonishing rise in student borrowing, it seems that the Millennial generation could be facing serious challenges. In essence, they may not prove to be the golden goose that many expected them to be. In an article entitled "Generation Nixed," Tavia Grant and Janet McFarland explain, "A generation of highly educated people that (the market) desperately needs to drive future growth isn't reaching its full potential. High debt and a late start in the job market means longer delays in buying houses, cars and appliances."[14]

Others, that I've spoken to, like Kit Yarrow, professor of consumer psychology and author of one of the seminal books on Millennial marketing, *Gen BuY*, see it quite differently. On the one hand, she readily acknowledges the unique circumstances that were foundational for Gen Y consumers and the troubles they face: "Gen Y'ers were children in an unprecedented era of economic prosperity. They received an average of five times the allowance of their parents. By the standards of any previous generation, and across every socio-economic group, this generation was indulged."

She is also quick to point out, however, that our habits and tendencies as young consumers often become entrenched and carry forward with us: "What people experience in their formative years typically becomes their baseline expectation for life. Those baseline expectations remain intact. What's changed is how Gen Y goes about satisfying them. I think they're leading the charge in forcing retailers to change. From in-store price comparisons to ganging up on companies to force fee changes, to "wardrobing" (buying, wearing and then returning) purchases, Gen Y is wily in looking for ways to get what they want for less. Retailers are going to have to stay nimble."[15]

And it's this "nimbleness" that Yarrow points to that could be the crux of the whole Millennial matter. They are more susceptible to change because they are exposed to more messages than any generation in history. They have more access to what's new. They have the tools and technology to make decisions without the help of brands and retailers. And much to the marketer's chagrin, they're infinitely smarter consumers than their parents were.

So, while few can claim to have Millennials completely figured out, it's safe to say that there are brands with common characteristics that have appealed to this generation. Apart from the table stakes of having a great product, brands that are winning with Millennials are:

- **authentic** like Lululemon, living what their brand espouses and being real;
- **purpose driven** like TOMS Shoes, supporting a human purpose beyond pure profit;
- **sensory** like Red Bull, injecting the brand with great media, live events and high-octane experiences;
- **quick to change** like Apple, constantly driving obsolescence with its latest products; and
- **socially savvy** like Zappos.com, nurturing the visibility of everyone in the company through social networks.

Ethnic Markets

When it comes to multicultural marketing, you might wonder what all the fuss is about. After all, America is the great *melting pot*, and Canada, the *cultural mosaic*, right? "Give me your tired, your poor, your huddled masses, etc." Hasn't marketing always been challenged with communicating to consumers across cultural and ethnic boundaries?

Relatively speaking, the answer is actually *no*.

Historically, immigration to both countries was restricted mostly to Western European nations. In fact, in 1924 the U.S. government enacted several pieces of legislation, including one called the Asian Exclusion Act, that were specifically aimed at limiting or restricting certain nationalities entirely—mainly Chinese, Indian, Southern and Eastern Europeans and individuals from the Middle East—from immigrating to the United States at all. According to the U.S. Department of State Office of the Historian, "In all of its parts, the most basic purpose of the 1924 Immigration Act was to preserve the ideal of American homogeneity."[16]

For its part, even the traditionally more liberal Canada shared a very similar approach, at one point even placing an openly discriminatory head tax on Chinese immigrants in the hope that it would quell their intent to migrate. Some thanks after the government used Chinese laborers to build much of the country's national railway system.

Amazingly, it wasn't until the mid-1960s—known in demographic circles as the *era of liberalization*—that both the United States and Canada removed all nationality and country-of-origin restrictions from their respective immigration policies.[17] And so, what we know today as the great melting pot of America and the cultural mosaic of Canada are, in historic terms, relatively new and unfamiliar places—places we're still fumbling around in.

If you're not already actively engaged in multicultural marketing, these are, no doubt, some of the statistics that are keeping you up at night.

In the United States:

• One in two births in 2011 were Hispanic children.

• The Hispanic market's buying power surpassed $1 *trillion* in 2011.

• The Hispanic population is expected to make up 23 percent of the population by 2050.

• Asians are expected to make up 10 percent of the population (or, 40.6 million) by 2050.

In Canada:

• In the 2006 census, more than 200 unique ethnic origins were reported.

• Two-thirds of population increase in Canada is a result of immigration.

- It's projected that 63 percent of the population of Toronto and 59 percent of Vancouver will belong to visible minorities by 2031.
- In 2006, only 49 percent of residents in the city of Vancouver listed English as their mother tongue.
- By 2031, as many as one-third of Canadians will belong to a visible minority.

If, on the other hand, you're well underway with your multicultural marketing effort, you're probably already seeing some of these very positive realities:

- Although hit heavily by the recession, Hispanic consumers are less likely than most to carry large amounts of mortgage or credit card debt.
- Hispanics now make up the fastest-growing consumer segment in the luxury category.
- Six in ten Asian immigrants have a bachelor's degree.
- Asians have a lower incidence of poverty than the U.S. national average, and higher-than-average household income.
- According to a Pew Research Center report: "Asian Americans are the highest-income, best-educated and fastest-growing racial group in the United States. They are more satisfied than the general public with their lives, finances and the direction of the country, and they place more value than other Americans do on marriage, parenthood, hard work and career success."[18]
- Fifty-two percent of immigrants to Canada purchased a home within two years of their arrival.[19]

Yet despite the clear arithmetic that underscores the rewards of connecting with large ethnic consumer groups, multicultural marketing remains a mere bolt-on in many companies—an afterthought to their mainstream marketing programs and structures, something they feel they can check off the list with the odd Cinco de Mayo sale or Year of the Dragon promotion.

For those retailers, there's another key point they need to be cognizant of (and, frankly, it's the only one that really matters). It is this: *companies that do not make multiculturalism a genuinely informed, sincere and integrated priority will become irrelevant and will vanish from the market.* Maybe not this quarter or this year but eventually and likely sooner than you think.

You see, the math is pretty straightforward. Immigration is the *only* thing propping up our modest population growth, and even at the present rate of entry, both the U.S. and Canadian populations are set to begin shrinking—the United States by 2048, and Canada as early as 2031. The cause is twofold. First, as discussed earlier, we're simply having too few children. Second, despite new immigrants being younger and having higher fertility rates on average, there simply aren't enough of them to backfill the domestic fertility deficit. And contrary to the notion that immigration is escalating out of control, it isn't. It's actually declining. You read that correctly: *fewer* people are coming to our shores.

Chapman University professor and expert on demographics Joel Kotkin summed it up as follows: "One cause for concern is rapid decline in immigration, both legal and illegal. Although few nativist firebrands have noticed, the number of unauthorized immigrants living in the U.S. has decreased by 1 million from 2007. Legal immigration is also down. Meanwhile, the number of Mexicans annually leaving Mexico for the U.S. declined from more than 1 million in 2006 to 404,000 in 2010—a 60% reduction."[20]

So, contrary to what some factions might have you believe, the really scary problem isn't that we experience too *much* immigration—it's that we have too little! The inevitable consequence of which becomes too few income earners, too few taxpayers and too few consumers! Rest assured, this is not something that eludes our elected officials, so one can expect that we will indeed see government doing whatever is necessary to bolster immigration and, in doing so, support the tax base.

Therefore, brands had better prepare themselves for an even greater percentage of population growth and the resulting consumer outlays that will be generated by non-white Americans. This multicultural marketing imperative has escalated to become quite binary: make your brand or business meaningful to ethnic markets or go out of business. It's just that simple.

Employment

Bestselling business author Seth Godin characterizes our current economic turmoil as the onset of what he calls a "forever recession." Unlike normal, cyclical economic downturns, Godin suggests that what we have really encountered is the end of an era in which "good people could make above-average pay for average work." He suggests that we've arrived at "the end of the industrial age." The days of getting a modest education, securing a good job, following the rules and retiring with a tidy pension are simply over. Done.[21]

One can't help but notice that the numbers appear to bear him out completely. The post-recession economy has, in fact, been disproportionately adding back two kinds of employment: high-skilled, high-paying jobs, and low-skilled, low-paying jobs. The "average" jobs in the middle are disappearing.

Across the entire U.S. labor market, the Bureau of Labor Statistics points to only two categories of employment that are outstripping all others in terms of their post-recession contribution of jobs (see Table 3.2). They are *professional and related*

Table 3.2   U.S. Employment Recovery Since 2010.

	Percent of Market	Percent of Job Gains
Highest-Paying Jobs	15	20
Middle-Income Jobs	40	34
Lowest-Paying Jobs	40	46

Source: *Financial Post* April 11, 2012.

occupations (jobs that require significant education, training and skill) on the one hand, and *service* jobs (jobs that require little or no education, training or skill) on the other. The average middle-skilled worker—the paper pusher, ticket taker, assembly-line worker, middle manager—has been replaced by a machine or is now doing the work that two people did a decade ago. And anyone out there who is still doing average, low-skill work had better know that somewhere there's a robot being built to do what they do. The average middle-income worker, like the white Bengal tiger, is on the brink of extinction.

Clearly, this is horrible news for the millions of businesses in America who have thrived by delivering an average product or experience to average people.

Urbanization

Since at least the early 1970s, urban planners, sociologists, environmentalists and citizens have vehemently opposed what were rampant levels of suburban sprawl. Through the 1980s and 1990s, experts argued that power centers were a destructive force for the community, the environment, the small business base, municipal coffers, workers and, yes, even consumers. But all of this whining and complaining took a back seat because, above all else, suburban sprawl was a blessing for big retail: cheap land, favorable construction conditions, plenty of available labor and smooth transportation and supply-chain operations. It was retail heaven!

And there was one other thing about this sprawl that was fantastic. It made consumers easy to corral and control! Neighborhoods were neatly defined and demarcated, usually with a clear retail-development hub.

And planning where to put those stores was pretty simple too. It was all mapped out for you. If you were Home Depot, for example, all you needed to do was look at the five-year plans for towns and villages outside the city core, pick the ones reaching a critical mass of population and build a massive store there. You'd lose money for a year or two and then cash in once the newly built houses began filling. By that time you were already building the next store five or ten miles away. In the meantime, every little family owned and operated lumberyard in your circle of doom would have gone under, leaving the entire market ripe for the picking. This system of growth worked for a good 25 years and produced tens of thousands of big-box stores across every category imaginable.

Today, a debate rages about the future of suburbia, and particularly the power-center format. Some argue that we'll see a mass exodus from the suburbs as families make their way back to urban centers in the years ahead, while others don't buy the argument that a family can be raised in a downtown condo.

What we have in the way of evidence on both sides is largely anecdotal at this point. Some, like University of Michigan professor Christopher Leinberger, suggest that rising demand for urban real estate suggests a move by retiring boomers to urban centers to avail themselves of close proximity to health care, public transportation and entertainment. He also notes that Millennials are choosing cities for their job availability and excitement. Leinberger is far from being the only one projecting this downtown boomer migration.

Others, though, see boomers going the other way, moving even farther from urban congestion to enjoy the peace and quiet of rural communities. They also predict that Millennials will be likely to reach an age when they too prefer an unpolluted night sky to starless cities.

The more moderate view, and the one I subscribe to, is that we will soon witness cities beginning to look more like suburbs and suburbs beginning to look more like cities. Both will become more livable and sustainable places with people more able to rely on technology (not automobiles) to perform their work. Suburban, exurban and even rural communities will become more adapted to older citizens. Likewise, cities will become safer, quieter and cleaner places that better accommodate the aging residents who can afford to live there. Neither locale can operate without acknowledging the needs of an aging population—it's just too big a percentage of the population to ignore.

In either scenario, retail will be required to adapt accordingly—and it will. In the suburbs we're already beginning to see more mixed-use development and walkable, small-format retailing. In cities, we're beginning to see the transformation of big-box retail as it shoehorns into smaller, more "shopable" spaces that are adjacent to eateries, entertainment venues and transit. In both cases, we're seeing government holding retailers to higher standards for aesthetics, community involvement and economic return.

What seems increasingly out of place is the vast, asphalt wasteland of power centers. And to that point, retailers like Best Buy are now struggling to find ways to make their retail space productive. Home Depot is selling off unused parking lot space, and even Target has begun experimenting with in-store licensing to local merchants. While it may not be dead, it's safe to say that the big-box, as a model, has seen its zenith. It just doesn't make sense anymore.

As far back as 2008, *Big Box Reuse* author Julia Christensen began documenting the closures of big-box retail formats around the United States as well as the creative ways that municipalities were repurposing them to become productive community spaces. Big-box stores are being reclaimed as day care facilities and museums—and even churches!

The decline of the model also means an end to many of the efficiencies and cost savings that came with it. Large retailers will once again have to fight in close proximity, where much of their heavy artillery is useless to them.

THE END OF THE C+ WORLD

Average used to be what all consumers aspired to. Consequently, it was what all retailers aspired to deliver, and for more than 60 years they did just that. They sold average things to average people, at average prices in average stores, and did it all with average levels of service. In essence, they aimed for a C+, and that put them at the head of the class because it was a C+ world. Today, households are diverse, preferences are disparate, trends move like lightning and expectations at retail are higher—much higher.

Today, C+ is a failing grade. There is no such thing as an average or typical consumer. And regardless of what you do or what you sell, the days of winning by being average are over.

4

The Broken Funnel

TRY THIS: take a look at the brand images below and see what pops into your head.[1]

I'm willing to bet that each of these logos almost instantaneously conjured up the brand names Tony the Tiger, Mr. Clean, Kentucky Fried Chicken (KFC) and Maytag. Depending on your age, you might have struggled a little with one or two. But for the most part, you probably had very little trouble recognizing them, right? Good.

Now try naming the two people you see here.[2]

Nothing coming to mind? Not a clue? Don't worry, you're not alone. Of the thousands of people to whom I've posed this question in sessions both in the United States and Canada, only one person has *ever* immediately recognized these two men.

They are James Watson and Francis Crick, two of the three scientists who are credited with discovering DNA—the essential building block of all known life on earth. Now, while this little discovery might not be as meaningful to some as a bowl of sugary breakfast cereal or a bucket of finger lickin' good chicken, it's still somewhat disconcerting that we don't recognize two men who arguably changed the course of modern science and medicine, but we do immediately recognize a fictional feline and a bald clean freak.

However, this actually makes perfect sense. Because as brilliant as Watson and Crick might have been, they made one big mistake that will likely forever have them taking a back seat to Mr. Clean and Colonel Sanders. Their mistake? you ask. They simply didn't buy enough television advertising, of course!

THE ERA OF THE BRAND

The fact is that for almost 100 years, brands have managed to pump their logos, taglines and jingles into our temporal lobes. Some of the most recognizable images in popular culture are actually branded images. Sadly, most of this has nothing at all to do with the uniqueness, quality or performance of the products themselves. It wasn't as though Mr. Clean was lightning in a bottle; on the contrary, it was an average product for average households. Its success, like the success of so many other brands, was directly attributable to something else — something far more powerful than Mr. Clean could ever hope to be. The meteoric ascent of these and so many other brands of the era was the result of a new ballistic marketing weapon: mass media.

"What you call love was invented by guys like me to sell nylons."

— *Don Draper, Mad Men*

Long before Howard Stern was self-anointed "king of all media," there was another king. Its name was Television. Consider this: in 1950, 9 percent of households owned a television. By 1965, that figure had rocketed to over 92 percent. Moreover, in the same time period, households increased their viewing time by 25 percent! Television spread like wildfire, reaching the 50-million-household mark in a third of the time it took radio to reach the same status. And, above all else, it was television that breathed new life into nineteenth-century marketing theorist Elias Lewis's classical marketing model, known as the *purchase funnel*.

Lewis maintained that in order for brands to be successful, they needed to first and foremost build *consumer awareness*. Once they had generated that awareness, they needed to convert it into *interest* about their product. When that was achieved, they then had to build *desire* on the part of the consumer to actually *want* what the brand was selling. Doing this enough would eventually catapult at least a percentage of those consumers to the final stage of the funnel, which he called *action*, where the consumer actually buys the product or service.

The Purchase Funnel

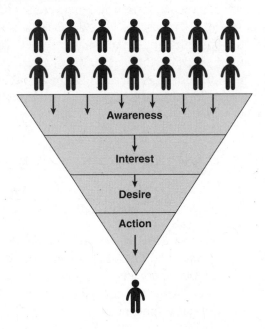

For close to a century the purchase funnel stood as the model by which marketing was executed. And winning was pretty simple—with all other things being equal, those who poured the most marketing impressions into the top of the funnel would win the most customers at the bottom of the funnel. It was a numbers game, pure and simple.

What made things doubly fantastic for brands and retailers was the sheer predictability of how, when and where the consumer's path to purchase would unfold. Like mice through a maze, there was only one way for consumers to move successfully through the buying process and get to the *cheese*, so to speak—and marketers knew it like the back of their hand.

Because of the enormous audience sizes for what was, at the time, only a handful of scheduled shows, television afforded marketers unprecedented capability to build widespread and immediate awareness. In fact, television was so effective as a medium that, in 1965, if you wanted to reach 80 percent of the viewing public, you needed only to run three commercials in primetime. Three! Just run a few ads during *Lassie*, *My Favorite Martian* or *Gunsmoke* and you were pretty much guaranteed instant awareness. There was no longer any need to guess where the average consumer was or how to reach them with a print ad or radio message. Scheduled television programming with limited shows meant that marketers knew with deadly accuracy exactly where to reach consumers—and how.

Once you'd captured the consumer's awareness, television also gave wide creative latitude to build interest. Product demonstrations and celebrity endorsements were just a couple of the tactics designed to develop consumer interest, and they worked. After all, if Pat Boone drove a Chevy, "Shouldn't I too?" consumers wondered.

Next came the job of building desire, which in most cases was quite simple. At that time, one of the most effective means of doing this was simply by making extraordinary claims— about either the performance or the popularity of the product. Kellogg's Corn Flakes, for example, ran ads calling itself the "world's favorite" cereal. Whether that claim was true or not was hardly the point. The question is, how could anyone have proved it to be false? In fact, short of getting the local news media involved, consumers had no real means of corroborating anything that marketers said. That meant they had to buy the product to see for themselves, and as you can imagine, that was just fine with retailers! Companies were largely unabated in what they claimed. And some of those claims were pretty wild.

Scan this to see a bizarre early TV ad for Dorothy Gray face cream.

Lastly, of course, came the push to purchase, and in this regard there was largely only one choice—the local retail store. Sure, some sales might have gone through mail order, but the store was where most consumer traffic was being directed. Once in the store, the consumer, excited by false or exaggerated claims and with no real knowledge of product alternatives, often had little choice but to accept what he or she was being told and buy, buy, buy!

So, let's take stock of what retailers had going for them. Not only was the population expanding with middle-class families, most of whom were improving their financial lots and seeking largely the same sorts of products and services, but now brands had a one-way pipeline directly into their living rooms through television. And to top it all off, they could tell consumers pretty much whatever they needed to tell them to sell their products—most of which were entirely mediocre!

Yes, average products and services were the nails, and television became a God-given hammer. And all of it amounted to ringing registers and skyrocketing profits for retailers. It was tantamount to having a license to print money and that printing press ran smoothly for about 30 years.

By the early 1980s, however, this tidy little marketing model was becoming badly unhinged. Decades of increasingly liberal immigration policy, the sexual revolution, the human rights movement and polarizing economic policies had all worked to drastically alter the picture of the typical consumer. The Rockwellian image of American family life had begun to flake away, revealing a substrate of increasingly varied lifestyles, economic strata and consumer tendencies.

It was becoming clear that a one-size-fits-all approach to consumer marketing would simply no longer do.

Consequently, it was also at about this time that the vise-like grip of the big three television networks began to weaken. Cable networks started springing up, filling a growing need for niche programming that the big networks couldn't or wouldn't provide. The videocassette recorder (VCR) also made its commercial debut, giving consumers (who could afford one) newfound freedom to watch movies and other content at their leisure. It was becoming increasingly hard for brands to track down and corner consumers in TV land.

Television certainly wasn't alone in this havoc. Other forms of media also began fragmenting in response to demographic shifts. The magazine industry, once dominated by generalized, middle-class lifestyle publications began exploding with titles focused on cult interests, varying household income strata and fringe pastimes. Radio formats began moving away from pure Top 40–based formats to account for varied musical tastes, new formats and even language-based preferences.

As a result of this media fragmentation, the task of identifying clusters of largely identical consumers became far trickier. The broadening of programming choice steadily splintered the once large and homogeneous audience. As viewers, readers and listeners became harder to corral, major media rates began to soar, beginning a decades-long divergence between audience size and advertising rates. For brand advertisers it meant paying more to reach fewer and fewer people. Between 1972 and 2002, television advertising rates, for example, increased almost tenfold.[3]

Magazines felt the economic shift, too. While more magazines were being sold in absolute terms, title proliferation meant that circulation on a title-by-title basis was actually declining. By 1995, Hearst, one of America's largest magazine publishers, announced that it would cut circulation of 13 of its 15 magazines, but in turn would be raising advertising rates on remaining circulation. Again, advertisers were getting less and paying much more.

When advertising was cheap, no one really cared how many marketing bullets missed the target. But now, with exponentially higher costs to reach increasingly elusive consumers, brands adopted a hawk-like focus on results. It became obvious for many that a vastly different approach to marketing was required.

THE ERA OF THE RETAILER

Fortunately (or unfortunately) for brands, retailers meanwhile had made extraordinary piles of cash between the 1960s and the 1980s. By 1980, for example, Walmart reached the $1-billion sales mark. In 1981, Home Depot, which would prove to be the fastest-growing retailer in U.S. history, became a publicly listed company on the NASDAQ and later the New York Stock Exchange.[4] For its part, Target was on a decade-long acquisition spree—one that would see its influence spread well beyond the confines of the Midwest. By 1989, it had opened stores in the Carolinas, Texas, Colorado, California, Michigan, Nevada and Florida. It was also during the 1980s that we saw a highly successful retailer from Minnesota, called Sound of Music, change its name to Best Buy.[5] And, by 1988, in a move that would signify a new era, Walmart opened its first "super center" in Washington, Missouri.

And so it was…

Fueled by decades of inconceivable success, these and other chains grew to absolutely epic proportions with a proposition that was comprised of essentially two things: massive product selection and razor-sharp prices. I, for one, can clearly remember my first trip to a Home Depot and being completely dumbfounded at the sea of products in stock. It was unlike anything I had ever seen before. I and my fellow consumers were like kids in the proverbial candy store…awestruck.

As a consumer, it was this mountain of selection and tight focus on value that made the less desirable aspects of the big-box experience tolerable. With the pressure to keep up with the Joneses intensifying, and middle-income wages largely static, the lust for cheap stuff became so intoxicating that we accepted everything else that came with it: the driving to the dusty edge of town, the parking what seemed like a mile from the door, the walking through cavernous stores, the shuttering of Main Street merchants, the utter absence of service and the generally disengaged staff. We bought it all—lock, stock and *family-size* barrel!

This, of course, only fueled even greater retailer growth, which in turn put unprecedented power into the hands of retailers. Thus, many brands found themselves at the end of the very swords they had helped to forge! The retailers that they had helped to reach such unimaginable success were now turning on them. It was no longer the retailer that was reliant on brands to drive traffic to their doors, but rather the brands that depended on retailers for distribution and access to consumers. Things were turned on their heads.

This, of course, caused many brands to adopt an entirely different approach. In fact, by the mid-2000s, Procter & Gamble announced a strategy that it called "store-back," and hailed it as the future of retail marketing. In simple terms, store-back meant that every marketing campaign began by first establishing how it would execute in the store. Then, and only then, would the brand team work backwards to what the media creative and executional plan might look like to support the in-store components of the project. In essence, *everything* started at the store!

For many industry analysts though, subtext of the store-back strategy was clear: after more than 80 years, the relationship between brands and their retailers (particularly big ones) had reversed entirely. Where only a few decades earlier saw brands calling the shots, it was now the retailers who gave the orders. No single label or vendor was more powerful than Walmart. No single brand came before the Home Depot brand. The retailer was now the dog and the brands it carried nothing more than fleas, along for the ride.

The retailer/vendor balance of power had shifted. Retailers developed very different expectations of the brands they carried. Namely that the brands (not the retailer) be responsible for making sure they sold their products through — or else. Retailers would not tolerate being loaded up with products only to have them sit on shelves while advertising folks sipped brandy and smoked Montecristos. Nope, the onus was on the brands to do whatever they needed to do to maintain shelf space with retailers who seemed remarkably comfortable kicking them to the curb if necessary.

There was a new king: the retailer.

As time passed, brand manufacturers that were once the beneficiaries of retailer growth were increasingly becoming victims of it. It was not uncommon for vendor brands to be required to pay their big-box customers huge sums for new store openings, provide ongoing marketing funds, give deep promotional price points, accept the return of non-selling goods, build specially requested displays or signage and be forced to pay steep financial penalties for failing to ship orders on time or in full. For some brands, their relationship with big-box retail became like an abusive marriage. It was a relationship that while brutal and soul crushing, accounted for too much of their annual figures to give up. And if they did give up, surely another vendor, perhaps as far away as Asia, would be more than happy to take their place.

———

ENTER THE INTERNET

It was at about this time that the terms "World Wide Web" and "Internet" began to wend their way into mainstream business conversations. What began as a complex "network of networks" was, by the early 1990s, becoming suitable for commercial and consumer applications. Mosaic, which would later be renamed Netscape Navigator, made the seemingly limitless geography of the web navigable — even by us mere mortals.

Many marketers and consumers, however, struggled at first to find the relevance of what appeared to most to be nothing more than a bunch of disparate computers around the world, somehow strung together by means few could fathom. Most companies saw the Internet as nothing more than a one-way information highway, where they, along with thousands—perhaps millions—of other brands, could do not much more than erect a digital billboard. Many couldn't even conceive of how they would be discovered by consumers in this digital labyrinth.

Some, like Internet commercialization pioneer Ken McCarthy, very clearly recognized the unprecedented capabilities that the Internet would afford anyone who manufactured, created or developed any kind of good or service. It was McCarthy, too, who called out the fact that because manufacturers naturally seek to produce what sells most widely, they don't always manufacture the *best* product, but rather the product that best fits specific cost parameters based on anticipated demand. In other words, average products were by default produced for mass consumption. The Internet, he surmised would allow for the creation and sale of far more extraordinary products, which although designed for smaller markets, could be sold as effectively as mass produced goods. And where most brands had been using a *one-to-many* approach for the last 80 or so years, a personalized approach to selling was once again possible.

Scan this to watch a video of the first Internet marketing conference.

Others, like *Wired* magazine editor-in-chief Chris Anderson, have since expanded on McCarthy's early vision, pointing to the Internet's unprecedented ability to serve niche markets—the "long tail," as he called it. No longer were brands bound to selling what was most popular or what would sell through mass markets. Thousands or perhaps even millions of products, while being less popular or less suited to the masses, could now be sold to consumers for whom they were relevant and valued.

At the time of the first Internet marketing conference in 1994, there were approximately 40 million Internet users worldwide. Today, a mere 19 years later, the metrics are simply staggering.

- As of 2012, there are more than 2.5 billion Internet users worldwide.[6]
- From 1997 to 2010, Internet advertising revenue soared 2,788 percent from $900 million to $26 billion.[7]
- As of March 2011, there were 644 million active websites.[8]
- A casual search of Amazon.com for books suggests the site has over 44 million items available.
- U.S. online retail sales topped $200 million in 2011, making up about 7 percent of total retail sales.[9]

Despite the clear trend here, some marketers and retailers I speak to insist on pointing out that online sales constitute a relatively small percentage of total retail. They cling as well to the desperate hope that what they sell requires too much touch and feel by consumers to make it a viable web sale.

To first address the numbers—yes, online retail is currently about 7 to 8 percent of total retail. However, that figure has been growing by double-digit percentages, while retail growth in general has been relatively flat. Regardless of how many sales are currently made online, the percentage will soon be far too significant to ignore or minimize. In fact, at its current average rate of annual growth, online retail could reach upwards of 30 percent of total retail sales within a decade.

As for the consumer needing to touch and feel what you sell, I will offer this:

- Online retailer Zappos.com sold over a billion dollars' worth of clothing and footwear that no one tried on before buying.
- By as early as 2006, eBay had sold its 2-millionth passenger vehicle without pre-buy test drives.[10]
- In 2010, online wine sales grew by 38 percent.[11]
- The California town of Bridgeville was auctioned for 1.75 million dollars on eBay.

So, at the risk of sounding overly cocky, if someone can buy a town in California online, I'm pretty sure I can find and buy whatever you sell online, too.

And for the tougher stuff, technology is giving us the ability to see and experience products in a virtual way before we buy. From seeing how furniture will look in my home to how eyeglass frames will look on my face, digital technology has given us the means to try before we buy, and all without ever setting foot in a store.

In essence, the Internet has quickly become the biggest big-box of them all, redefining our entire concept of convenience and product selection forever. All of a sudden, Walmart, Home Depot and other hyper-retailers don't look so big anymore.

ENTER THE NETWORK

Almost a decade after the early commercialization of the Internet, yet another conference in San Francisco took place, this time hosted by O'Reilly Media and focusing on something that was being called "Web 2.0." What transpired over three days in October 2004 was a discussion of the future vision of the Internet, and how it would not remain a static repository of institutionally catalogued information, but rather become an open platform for creation, sharing and collaboration.

In summing up Web 2.0, *Time* magazine writer Lev Grossman said this:

It's a story about community and collaboration on a scale never seen before. It's about the cosmic compendium of knowledge Wikipedia and the million-channel people's network YouTube and the online metropolis MySpace. It's about the many wresting power from the few and helping one another for nothing and how that will not only change the world, but also change the way the world changes.[12]

In short, what Tim O'Reilly, founder of O'Reilly Media, and others saw was the potential for the Internet to become largely the *domain of the people*—and not of institutions or brands. People would not only become the consumers of information but, more importantly, they would become the producers, authors and creators on a scale the world had never seen before. And this incredible wealth of content would be shareable within open networks based on community and collaboration.

What flowed out of this thinking, of course, quite literally changed the world forever. What we later came to know as "social media" would rewrite the rules on just about every aspect of life, including how we connect with friends, share ideas, elect heads of state, overthrow heads of state, find jobs, lose jobs, find houses, find spouses, leave spouses, find new spouses, find pets, locate lost pets, entertain ourselves, entertain others, celebrate birthdays, memorialize deaths and, yes, even shop.

Suddenly, with one simple search, everything I ever wanted to know about a product was there for the taking. But it wasn't just stuff the *brand* wanted me to know, it was what other users, people just like me, thought about the product—reviews from real people who had actually put the product or service to use. If something was awesome, they could tell me about it. If it sucked, I could know that too—and not after I bought the product, but before I opened my wallet! And if I had questions, I could ask them.

In only a few short years, the web went from being a big bulky encyclopedia to becoming a lightning-fast global conversation. And, within that conversation, consumers could self-select communities according to their passions! If I was crazy about auto repair, I could join an auto repair community. If cosmetics were more my thing, there was a community for that too. It made no difference how niche the interest, somewhere there was a community dedicated to it! In essence, consumers were self-segmenting according to their interests and doing it on a scale never seen before.

In a remarkably short time, the bulk of information on the Internet went from being institutionally generated to user generated. Media was no longer a one-way conduit for institutions to deliver messages to the public. Instead, it had become a multidirectional dialogue where the audience had as much volume (or more) as the brand.

Zuck's Law:
"Every year people share twice as much online."
— *Mark Zuckerberg*

The following is perhaps one of the clearest leading indicators of this revolution: In February of 2012, Procter & Gamble (P&G) announced a $10-billion restructuring effort — only the second in its 175-year history. Among other things, the plan included cutting marketing staff and executing a very clear shift away from television media in favor of more targeted digital forms of marketing. To be clear, the company that had practically *invented* mass marketing on television was all but throwing in the towel on it.

But this isn't meant to degenerate into a debate about old media versus new, or which formats are winning and which are losing — that's really not the point. As we'll see, all media formats are in a state of flux and integration. Rather, I look at this move by P&G as perhaps the clearest admission that the era of mass, industrialized marketing has come to an abrupt close.

And as for Elias Lewis's once-reliable purchasing funnel, it now seems somewhat rusted and broken beyond repair. The rules of generating *awareness, interest, desire* and *action* have clearly changed forever.

Awareness can no longer be easily, inexpensively and broadly gathered. In fact, reaching the same 80 percent of prime-time viewers (which once took a mere three commercials) would now require 117 primetime ad spots. That's assuming you don't get time-shifted, DVR'd or TiVo'd. I don't know of a single brand that can afford a media spend of that magnitude. Moreover, with the average consumer being exposed to upwards of 3,000 marketing messages per day, new tools are enabling them to sift, sort and select options that are relevant to their needs. Consumers no longer need retailers to tell them what they should want. And, most importantly, in a world of infinite choice, even if they do see the ad, who knows if they'll actually give it a second thought.

Interest in products can no longer be ignited with meaningless product attributes, exaggerated claims or even gratuitous celebrity endorsements. Consumers have the power to validate or eviscerate any manufacturer information or claim with just a few clicks. Where the consumer of the 1960s lived, by today's standards, in a dark vacuum, today's shopper can often possess more information about a product than the people who actually make it. Shoppers are increasingly connected to what's happening and to one another, relying more on the advice of strangers than claims of advertisers.

Desire is not something that can be fabricated simply by leading customers to believe they're the only ones missing out! The shopper's entire network of friends and colleagues is at their fingertips. If they want to know what their friends like, they can ask them—all of them—instantly! And because the goal of the new consumer is not to be "average"—not to be like their friends but to be different—the popularity pitch that worked so well in the 1960s and 1970s is a dead end. Consumers don't want what everyone else has; rather, they want what their friends don't even know exists!

Action, in the form of sales, can no longer mean systematically driving customers to retail stores. There's only one place that most consumers go first, and it's called Google. If you're lucky enough to win the Google page listing battle and actually get a consumer into your brick-and-mortar store, just watch that they don't end up buying from a competitor while they're there, using the computer they brought in their pocket.

Increasingly, there is no defined and predictable path to purchase. No cognitive checkpoint that brands and retailers can patrol. No one channel of media wide enough to carpet-bomb an entire market. And, most importantly, no amounts of marketing spend great enough to change any of this.

THE END

If it sounds as though I've painted a picture of a horrible future for brands and retailers, I can assure you that, for many, it will be the reality. Some simply won't make the transition. Those that will be particularly challenged include any business that

- feels the best way to reach the right consumer is in large, broadly defined segments;
- believes it can sell using exaggerated performance and half-truths and get away with it;
- is depending on brand names and conventional media to bring customers to its door;
- believes what it sells cannot be purchased online;
- feels product selection and price alone can make it viable in the long run;
- works only to be *good enough* in all aspects of what it does; and

- designs a mediocre product or experience to appeal to *average* consumers.

On the other hand, the good news is this: for those who can make the transition, an absolute bonanza of opportunity awaits—a brand-new era in which size and scale of operation is no longer a clear advantage, deep pockets no longer a requisite for awareness. And brands no longer a guarantor of loyalty.

You see, there's a completely new reality that most brands and retailers are still not recognizing. Elias Lewis's funnel isn't defunct at all. It's just been completely reversed. The consumer is now the one who, if they feel your brand is worthy, has the power to broadcast on your behalf to their network and their possessive networks' network and so on. It's no longer about putting the most meaningless marketing impressions *into* the funnel but rather getting the most *meaningful* impressions *out* of the funnel. The consumer is now the most powerful form of media there is!

The sovereign reign of television, brands and big-box retailers has come to an end.

The king is dead. Long live the consumer!

Part II

The Beginning

5

The New Law of Average

I WAS RECENTLY IN Fort Worth, Texas, speaking to executives and managers who hailed from a large and diverse group of companies in the direct-selling industry—companies that sell a vast array of products either through in-home sales or direct-sale TV advertising. My talk centered on the enormous and ongoing challenges that brands and retailers face in winning consumer attention, given today's unprecedented level of media fragmentation, product proliferation and consumer empowerment. It was a full-on look at how the rules of reaching and relating with consumers are being completely rewritten. On the flip side, I was also quick to point out the novel rewards available to those brands that could rise to an entirely new level of understanding and performance.

Throughout the talk, I couldn't help but notice a middle-aged guy sitting off to one side of the room. He shifted nervously in his seat and listened intently with a decidedly pained expression on his face. I fully expected that at any moment he would head for the exit, but strangely enough he didn't. He stayed.

At the end of the session, several people came up to chat with me and share their thoughts on the presentation. Eventually, however, the room emptied—with one exception: the uncomfortable-looking guy!

He rose from his seat and approached the stage. He was a tall, well-dressed fellow, in what I would guess to be his early 50s. The pained expression he wore earlier had now given way to a pleasant smile as he stuck out his hand and introduced himself as Jim. He was the founder and CEO of one of the companies in attendance. He thanked me for the presentation, but quickly added that listening to it had made him feel physically ill. A little stunned, I immediately started running my mental movie reel of the presentation, wondering what I could possibly have said that would have made him (or anyone else, for that matter) feel sick! Inducing illness in one's audience is not often the going-in objective of most speakers.

Noticing my somewhat dumbfounded expression, he went on to explain.

"For years," he said, "I believed that my company was different and unique. That we were special. But as I sat and listened to your talk, it became more and more apparent to me that we had become nothing more than average— 'stuck in the middle,' to use your words. I realized that I was neither the most convenient brand to do business with nor the most extraordinary. There was nothing about us that stood out. It suddenly dawned on me that we were now just mediocre—and it literally made me sick."

Although I'd never heard it so plainly articulated, I was quite certain that what Jim felt that day in Texas was what thousands of retailers all over North America are feeling in the pit of their stomachs every day—that *something* very fundamental has changed, and that the world they knew had shifted on its axis just a little. The problem is that they can't put their finger on why or how. Sure, everyone knows there's a recession, but this feels deeper and farther-reaching.

And this feeling—this foreboding sense that average isn't good enough anymore—isn't a figment of our collective imagination. This is real. The market for mid-tier goods and services has indeed been shrinking, and it's not merely a condition brought on by recessionary forces. In fact, well before the collapse of 2008, firms like McKinsey & Company were tracking a precipitous decline in mid-tier consumer goods markets, with the five years between 1999 and 2004 seeing revenues in mid-tier companies trail the overall market by 6 percent annually. The recession hadn't caused the decline of the mid-tier, it only accelerated the damage that was already taking place.[1]

What Jim was feeling, whether he knew it or not, was that one of the most unusual, spectacular and sometimes worrisome periods in consumerism is coming to a rapid close, and the middle, now far from being where the action is, is in fact being gutted.

There is simply no more exploding population generating excess demand. In fact, population growth is now minimal, and what growth there was was largely the result of Hispanic and Asian immigration—which is also declining.

Gone is the burgeoning middle class with its minivans full of children and ever-improving standards of living. In fact, the middle class is losing economic ground and has been for decades. And now, even the colossal mountains of credit that had been compensating for the shortfall are being submerged in a sinking real estate market.

Gone are the cookie-cutter consumers who were all clamoring for the same things the Joneses had—the things retailers told them they needed if they were to be just like everyone else. The definitions of family, household and lifestyle have shifted beyond recognition, and so too have consumer needs, desires and preferences.

Gone are the surefire media pipelines of the twentieth century that used to pump average brand messages through to average consumers, who had no choice but to watch, listen, believe and ultimately buy. Consumers now have the means, data and wherewithal to compare, evaluate and acquire what they want, when they want it, wherever they want it. They, *not* the retailer and *not* the brand, are in the driver's seat.

And so, for Jim in Texas, and for thousands—perhaps millions—of businesses across North America, it all added up to one inevitable and apparently nauseating conclusion: the age of being successful by being average had come to a close. Average value propositions had essentially become invisible to consumers, who now would accept nothing less than clear and definitive value.

And what Jim realized that day that made him feel queasy was that he had to make a choice: either remain average and languish in the middle under constant threat of extinction, or swing for the fences and become remarkable in his category and thrive. It was that clear cut. That *in your face.*

All the evidence pointed to there being one way only to succeed as a brand, as a retailer, as *anything*, for that matter, and it was by creating such a strong gravitational pull around your business that consumers—like millions of energized atomic particles—would be drawn to you. No tricks, no gimmicks, no parlor games. Just pure awesomeness!

The remaining question, of course, is *how*?

"Nothing is so common-place as to wish to be remarkable."
— *Oliver Wendell Holmes, Sr.*

■■■■■

THE ROAD TO REMARKABLE

According to Kevin Maney, author of the book *Trade-Off: Why Some Things Catch On, and Others Don't*, the transformation begins with plainly understanding how all the forces I've shared with you have conspired to reshape the consumer market. What was once a robust middle-market is being replaced by a highly polarized consumer landscape with growing distance between what Maney calls high-fidelity and high-convenience experiences. As he explains, the mid-tier is rapidly drying up as consumers—and hence the entire retail market—bifurcates into these two realms of distinct value.

The distinction between these two value propositions is as follows:

High Fidelity	High Convenience
exclusive	ubiquitous
premium priced	low priced
limited availability/distribution	available through multiple channels/mass
concierge level of service	low service/self-service
niche appeal	wide appeal
consumer develops emotional connection	consumer forms cognitive connection

High-fidelity experiences and products, he maintains, are often more unique, cost more and tend to be more niche in nature. They are more exclusive and offer a higher level of quality, shopping experience and service. In other words, as Maney puts it, "fidelity is the *total experience* of something"—a brand, a retailer or a product—the sum total of price, service, merchandising, product quality and so on wrapped up into the feeling the consumer walks away with.

Convenience-based experiences, on the other hand, are comparatively ubiquitous, accessible and inexpensive. They are less about the experience and more about the sheer ease with which a product or service can be acquired.

The market space between these two extremes—what Maney calls *the fidelity belly* (marked in Figure 5.1 by a skull and crossbones)—is where a brand is neither high fidelity nor high convenience. This is where things get ugly in a hurry. I call it the intersection of *who* and *cares*. It's a space crowded with zombie brands lacking any clear and defined attributes or unique selling propositions. Without any readily apparent

High Fidelity

Figure 5.1   *High Fidelity versus High Convenience.*

value to capture consumer attention, they languish in the middle, dying a little more each day.

The belly is the pit of the market, where brands scratch and claw out an existence. It's a world of price matching, discounting and undercutting. It's the realm of continual brand compromises in the interest of survival. In a word, it's retail hell.

For the purpose of illustrating the model, we could plot the ultra-exlusive, by-appointment-only, Rodeo Drive showroom of Bijan Beverly Hills at the apex of the high-fidelity axis, and Amzon.com at the opposite extreme along the high-convenience axis. One is a promise that the experience will be exclusive, prohibitively expensive and wrapped in exquisite service, and the other is a promise that the experience will be easy, quick and reasonably priced. At the intersecting points (the dead zone), we would find brands like JCPenney, Sears, Best Buy and thousands of others—brands that are neither highly convenient, nor remarkable shopping experiences. In the middle, value is nebulous and uncertain, while at the extremes it's abundantly clear.

It's important, however, not to confuse these two states of fidelity and convenience with luxury and discount. That would be a gross oversimplification of the way the market is really polarizing. In fact, it is entirely possible for experiences to be high fidelity *without* being luxury, and high convenience *without* being discount. Consider a $2 cup of coffee bought at Starbucks versus spending $2 for a cup of coffee at Dunkin' Donuts. The cost is identical, but the product, service, in-store environment, location and convenience elements are entirely different. Starbucks delivers what many would consider a high-fidelity coffee experience, while Dunkin' Donuts is the master of the high-convenience coffee experience. One is not necessarily better or more relevant than the other—both models work. Similarly, most consumers do not regard Amazon.com as a discount retailer—even though its prices can often be lower than competitors. Both fidelity and convenience propositions can be extremely successful. The choice the consumer makes depends largely on his or her personal level of engagement with the product to begin with. For some consumers, coffee is coffee. For others, the experience enjoyed while drinking the coffee is what matters most, and is what they're paying for.

All of this is made somewhat more complex by the fact that consumer preferences and behaviors can't be neatly categorized by demographics or even psychographics the way they once could. There's no such thing as a pure high-fidelity shopper or a pure convenience shopper. The Nordstrom shopper who seeks high fidelity at 10:00 a.m. while shopping for a Cartier watch could be the same shopper who looks only for convenience at the local Target later that day when buying flip-flops for the beach. Age, income, attitudes and preferences have become markedly less reliable predictors of purchase behavior. In a world with a disappearing middle, value is being completely redefined and redistributed, and consumers are moving between the poles as their product needs and preferences dictate.

What is abundantly clear, however, is that these infinitely more thoughtful and tactical consumers are now consistently shunning average, mid-market retail propositions. They're aggressively saving money on the goods and services that *don't* matter so much to them in order to spend more lavishly on the things that *do*. Unless something holds readily apparent value, consumers are simply looking past it.

It's also crucial to understand that the vapid middle ground is dynamic. It's like a black hole that can draw unwitting brands into it over time. It's an ever-expanding dead zone. Today's high-fidelity brand can easily become sucked into the void unless there's a constant effort to resist its deadly gravity! Brands have to constantly reinforce their positions and push themselves further out along their chosen (fidelity or convenience) axis.

WHERE DOES YOUR BRAND LIVE?

So, the first and most important question that your company has to answer is: Where in this spectrum of value are you now, and where *should* you be positioned relative to competitors? Are you a high-fidelity or high-convenience brand?

I know it seems like a simple enough question. And you might feel that you and your team should be able to easily align on the answer. However, you'd be shocked at the number of businesses I work with where even their most senior leaders can't agree on the answer to this most basic of strategic questions. I've even seen *co-founders* of companies disagree about whether their brand plays in the convenience or fidelity space. Shouldn't the people who founded a company agree on its fundamental market positioning? But it is instances like this that highlight the extent to which brands can drift, evolve and lose their sense of self, often without even being aware of it.

However, until you achieve alignment on this central issue, nothing else really sits right. Brick-and-mortar and online store design, pricing, service formats, media choices, hiring—everything is rendered hit and miss without first knowing unequivocally whether your brand is *high fidelity* or *high convenience*.

Oh. And one other thing: you can't be both. You *can't be both* high fidelity and high convenience at the same time. It simply doesn't work. They are like opposing energy forces that cancel one another out. Products and services that are high fidelity are so because they are *not* high convenience and vice versa. Experiences that are rare cannot also be plentiful and common. Things that are exclusive cannot be inclusive simultaneously. Brands that attempt to chase this dual positioning—what Maney calls *the fidelity mirage*—put themselves in abject peril.

This is precisely what happened to Starbucks when, between 2002 and 2007, the company nearly tripled its number of stores. The brand that had once been super-exclusive and somewhat exotic was now becoming as common as dirt. This ubiquity began to erode sales. There was no more cachet in arriving at a meeting, Starbucks coffee in hand, when you could buy one in the local grocery store or airport. The carefully crafted elusiveness that made Starbucks special was gone. The very specific service dimension that Starbucks had done so much to train, cultivate and articulate was being steadily eroded and watered down. Starbucks was ceasing to be special, and customers were noticing.

Upon his return as Starbucks chief executive in 2008, Howard Schultz's first orders of business included shuttering over 900 locations. Apart from pruning underperforming locations, Schultz's aim was to apply renewed focus on maintaining a unique customer experience—to reclaim what made the company unique in the first place. In order to recoup fidelity, the brand had to give up convenience. One could argue that in some cities like New York there are still far too many Starbucks locations, which detracts from the brand's equity.

Businesses intent on pursuing both positions would also be wise to consider the near-death experience of the Lacoste brand. Lacoste was founded in 1933 by René Lacoste and André Gillier after Lacoste—a tennis player—won the 1927 Davis Cup wearing what is now the famous embroidered alligator on his court blazer. For decades the brand enjoyed high levels of exclusivity and limited its distribution. To wear

Lacoste made you unique and special. During the 1970s and 1980s, however, after entering into an American licensing agreement with IZOD, the once-hard-to-come-across brand became severely overexposed, accessible and increasingly commoditized. This increased market penetration meant that you could buy Lacoste almost anywhere, and very often on sale. Thus, what had been a high-fidelity brand was now ho-hum and sapped of much of its glorious brand heritage and equity. After selling back its stake to Lacoste in 1993, IZOD as a manufacturer closed up shop. Today, the feisty Lacoste alligator is scratching and clawing its way back into the high-fidelity space through carefully managed distribution and branding.

Despite cases like this, many brands still insist on attempting to be all things to all people. Recently, for example, über-luxe department store Neiman Marcus and "cheap-chic" retailer Target announced that they would enter into a holiday co-promotion that would have both selling a collection of similar products at identical prices. The assumed motivation, as pricing expert Paul Hunt points out, is that "the retailers appear to be working towards mutually beneficial goals: first, to expand Neiman Marcus's range of customers, particularly among younger and less-affluent shoppers, and second, to retain Target's customers through association with the Neiman Marcus name and 'glow.'"[2] The question many are asking is, *at what price*? What incalculable damage could be done to the Neiman Marcus brand if its customers sense that it is becoming less exclusive, less ultra-premium and less what they bought into in the first place? Similarly, what harm could Target sustain if its loyal customers perceive the brand as becoming less inclusive, less *cheap-chic* and simply more *chic*—perhaps even a little *snooty*?

"In order to be irreplaceable one must always be different."

—*Coco Chanel*

GETTING OUT OF THE MIDDLE

Most retailers are not Neiman Marcus or Target. And more often than not, when I work clients through this model of positioning, they find themselves enormously conflicted. They come to the somewhat depressing conclusion that they are neither entirely high fidelity nor are they completely high convenience. They're a bit of both. And in a world with an evaporating middle, that leaves them vulnerable and open to attack from all sides.

The paramount question is, how *can* brands avoid being caught in the middle? What can they do to establish a beachhead in their category that's distinct and defendable? Moreover, if a brand does find itself being sucked into the void of "averageness," how can it jettison itself back to safer ground?

I've come to the conclusion that there are five competitive corners in any market that offer retailers a sustainable competitive advantage.

The Five Corners

While I was attending school in Montreal in the mid-1980s, a friend asked me out to lunch and suggested we go to a little restaurant called Wilensky—a family-owned place in an area of the Plateau-Mont-Royal called Mile End. I'd never heard of it but he assured me I'd like it.

When I arrived at Wilensky, the first thing I noticed was the disproportionate relationship between the tininess of the restaurant and the sheer enormity of the lineup waiting to get in. It was like a python trying to squeeze through a keyhole. I was told this was a pretty common sight. The business was open six days a week (they weren't open Sundays), and neighborhood residents, business people and tourists alike piled into what was literally no more than a hole in the wall.

Once you passed the threshold, however, it was like stepping into a time machine. Wilensky had remained largely the same since the 1930s, with a classic diner counter, stools and even the original push-button—*ca-ching*—cash register. There were no menus because, frankly, you didn't need them. There were only half a dozen choices of things to eat. You could have a hot dog, or a fried bologna and salami sandwich. If you preferred something cold, you could have an egg salad or cheese sandwich. That was it. If you had ordered the fried salami and bologna sandwich, it was served with mustard. If you didn't like mustard, well, you needed to find a different place to eat, because the mustard was mandatory—no exceptions. There were only a few choices of soda to drink and they were all mixed by hand, just as they had been when the place opened in 1932. There was very little room to sit, so most people simply stood and ate. Some took their meals with them.

So to be clear: you line up, any day but Sunday when it's closed, to get into a crowded restaurant with a pitiful level of choice only to have mustard on your sandwich whether you like mustard or not, and you can't even sit down to eat. Sounds pretty horrible, doesn't it? Well, it's not. In fact, it's brilliant. The line moves quickly, and the limited menu makes ordering simple. The food is delicious (and, yes, the mustard does make it even better) and it's cool to watch them mix the sodas. And the atmosphere…well, it's so memorable that I'm writing about it almost 30 years later. That's pretty remarkable in itself!

The secret to Wilensky's success is as simple as it is complex. For every person like me who loved it, I have no doubt that as many would walk out and would never return, because Wilensky is not for everyone. I have little doubt that Wilensky's owners not only realize this but also nurture it. The experience I had wasn't accidental. Each element of it was a choice that was made and refined over decades—the lineup, the decor, the menu, the mandatory mustard—all deliberate and by design. Wilensky was not trying to be all things to all people—far from it.

What Wilensky has done intuitively over more than 80 years is absolutely no different than what Apple, Virgin, Red Bull and many other great modern brands have done. They didn't try to be good at everything, but rather excellent at one thing only. They defined their corner of the market and went deep into it. This, of course, runs contrary to what most companies set out to do. Most want to do everything equally well, and in doing so appeal to the largest possible market segment. Everyone wants to be popular and broadly successful.

This tendency on the part of retailers to want to be good at everything was the subject of the 2001 book *The Myth of Excellence*—a work that is every bit as relevant today as it was when it was written. What authors Ryan Mathews and Fred Crawford contend is that there are five common attributes that all businesses compete on: product, price, service, ease of access and customer experience (we'll talk more about customer experience later). Furthermore, after significant research, they discovered that the most successful brands were *not* excellent at everything. In fact, they weren't even excellent at a few things. What Mathews and Crawford found, without exception, was that truly successful brands were excellent at *one thing only*, while being substantially differentiated in one other aspect of their business. From Walmart to Neiman Marcus, the pattern was the same—excellent at one thing and highly differentiated in another.

The word *excellent*, however, didn't mean that a brand was merely good or even excellent *some of the time*. Being excellent meant that you substantially dominated the market in a specific competitive attribute, and you did so 24 hours a day, seven days a week. Domination meant that when consumers considered a particular competitive attribute, like service, for example, your brand would be top-of-mind. To *differentiate*, on the other hand, meant that you took a decidedly unique approach to one other competitive attribute. You did something in a tangibly different way that set you apart from competitors—so much so that your customers could see and feel and explain the unique quality. Provided that brands could achieve excellence in one competitive attribute and differentiation in another, there was no need for them to be anything more than on a par with competitors in all other respects.

So, in the case of Wilensky's restaurant, one could argue that the eatery sold a highly *differentiated* menu while offering an *excellent* one-of-a-kind service experience. As for the other competitive attributes, with limited store hours and long lineups, the restaurant certainly did not make the experience easy for its customers. And although their prices were reasonable, one could undoubtedly eat elsewhere for about the same amount or less. It was clear that Wilensky was focused on two things only: making unique food and selling it in a wholly remarkable way. Wilensky had, in effect, safely occupied one of what I call the five competitive corners.

Take Your Corner

So, what are the five corners that a retailer can safely occupy? Well, the answer starts with declaring which end of the fidelity/convenience spectrum you're playing in. For our purposes here, let's assume that everyone in your organization is in agreement on this aspect. If you've agreed that your brand is better suited to competing in the high-fidelity space, there are only two positioning options:

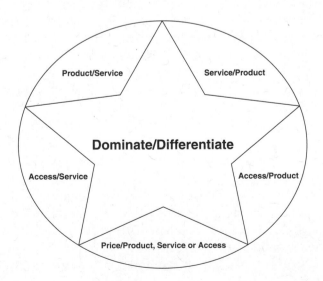

1. SELL REMARKABLE PRODUCTS IN A DIFFERENTIATED WAY

Companies like Walt Disney Parks and Resorts and Apple, for example, have a unique advantage in that they control the design and creation of the products they sell. This gives them ironclad control over design, quality and pricing. They create remarkable products that are, by any reasonable account, unique among market alternatives and have discernible, and in some cases patented, performance differences.

In and of itself, however, this manufacturing advantage isn't enough to guarantee a degree of immunity or safety. For example, Rubbermaid, which almost single-handedly defined the consumer plastic goods market, had a remarkable product. Nonetheless, the company experienced enormous troubles with distribution through big-box retail, succumbing to pricing and fulfillment issues. These tribulations led to the company being bought up in 1998. Today, Rubbermaid as a brand means very little. Merely having a remarkable product wasn't enough to make Rubbermaid's position in the market defendable or sustainable.

Apple and Walt Disney Parks and Resorts, however, not only make what they sell, the also serve it to consumers in a highly differentiated way. For example, unlike most theme parks, you will never see anyone transporting garbage at Disney. You will never see a "cast member" from Frontierland walking through Tomorrowland. You will never see maintenance crews traveling through the park. All of this is made possible by a network of tunnels underneath the parks, which Disney calls "utilidors" (utility corridors), that connect the entire park and even houses, shops, banks and cafeterias used by cast members. Where most companies might have stopped at creating an awesome product aboveground, Disney augmented it with a trademark level of service, made possible by tunnels underground.

The result for Apple, Disney and others like them is that even if someone could replicate their product, the likelihood that they could copy the nuances and systems that comprise the total brand offering is next to impossible.

But what if, unlike Disney or Apple, you *don't* manufacture what you sell? What if what you sell can be found and purchased elsewhere?

In reality, most retailers don't have the luxury of complete product exclusivity. Yet some are still wildly successful. These retailers have discovered the second competitive corner.

2. SELL DIFFERENTIATED PRODUCTS IN A REMARKABLE WAY

Spanish cycling shop Pavé doesn't manufacture what it sells. The store, located in Barcelona, carries a variety of bicycle brands across a range of manufacturers—which hardly seems like a reason to stand out in a world filled with cycling stores. Yet Pavé most definitely does. In fact, it's world-renowned.

Racing cycles, like sculpture, adorn the gallery-like interior of the Pavé Culture Cycliste store in Barcelona. (Image used with permission from Pavé Culture Cycliste.)

First off, the product assortment is highly differentiated, focusing exclusively on road-racing bicycles. No mountain bikes, BMX or trekking bikes—just road-racers. Secondly, it carries only the finest brands and models of road-racing bikes—the kind of stuff that makes a hardcore racer quiver in his or her spandex shorts! This highly curated and differentiated product assortment sets Pavé apart from competitors.

Where Pavé breaks the sound barrier, however, is in the way it sells these bikes. The immaculate, loft-style shop displays the bicycles like sculptures, each in its own backlit display. There's no clutter of product, no pollution of signage, no gear oil or sweat. It's clean, open and stunning. There's even a beautifully comfortable area where enthusiasts can relax, read magazines, chat and watch videos—all, of course, about the sport of cycling. One writer went so far as to call Pavé "an architect-designed, cathedral-like shrine to the tradition, lore and beauty of road-racing bicycles."[3] Clearly, it's not your typical cycling shop.

In essence, what Pavé did was narrow its market focus so as to exclude enormous groups of consumers that it had no interest in serving—a notion that is completely counterintuitive to most marketers who have been trained to chase the largest possible consumer segments with the most inclusive offerings they can find. However, by so precisely tailoring its assortment, and delivering it in a wholly unique and remarkable way, Pavé built a dominant and defendable position with its chosen market segment, which catapulted the company out of the void of the mid tier.

Along similar lines, green building-supply retailer TreeHouse in Austin, Texas, has carved out an equally unique position. First, it has chosen to sell a highly differentiated assortment of goods, focusing purely on products that are environmentally healthy, sustainable and socially responsible. Second, and more importantly, TreeHouse has created a remarkable way of selling these products by demystifying and simplifying the selection process for customers. Every product is rated according to a proprietary product filter, which allows customers to home in on products best suited to their personal criteria. TreeHouse also places an emphasis on customer education, deploying what it calls "slightly obsessed" in-store experts to educate customers on how their homes work so they can make fundamentally better decisions. What TreeHouse has created is a unique and defendable market position that sets it apart from others that simply *sell* green building products.

The Treehouse product filter demystifies the selection of environmentally
friendly building materials. (Courtesy TreeHouse, Inc.)

Suffice to say that neither Pavé nor TreeHouse will ever be
the next Walmart or Home Depot. And that, in effect, is precisely *why* their concepts are so competitively sustainable—
they are not mass-market propositions. However, they will be
exceptionally relevant and valuable to a smaller group of pas-
sionately engaged consumers.

Both of these high-fidelity positions are strong, defendable and sustainable corners of the fidelity space. Clearly,
though, not every retailer will be suited to competing in the
fidelity space. Some retailers are by definition better suited
to or more viable competing at the convenience end of the
spectrum.

For these retailers, there are three safe corners.

3. OFFER REMARKABLE EASE OF ACCESS WITH DIFFERENTIATED
SERVICE   When Amazon.com opened its online doors in 1994,
many believed the business wouldn't make it through its first
year, much less become one of the world's largest retailers.

Part of Amazon's success was a result of bringing consumers a new and remarkable level of access to an incredible and growing range of products—a trait that even today the company continues to expand upon. Surprisingly, however, many loyal Amazon customers point to *service* as one of the primary things that keeps them going back. By using advanced web analytics and sophisticated recommendation engines, Amazon has been able to go far beyond simply providing anytime, anywhere online access to the things that consumers want. It has also successfully differentiated itself from other online sellers with a distinct service dimension. It makes for a powerful combination.

4. OFFER REMARKABLE EASE OF ACCESS WITH DIFFERENTIATED PRODUCTS By almost any standard, 7-Eleven store locations are remarkably convenient. This ease of access via store location is a clearly dominant trait. On its own, however, making it easy for customers to find you isn't a guarantee of success. Plenty of stores in good locations go bankrupt. So, what is it exactly that makes 7-Eleven work?

The answer is something most customers wouldn't even be conscious of. In 2005, the company embarked on an effort with its franchisees to better understand the unique customer preferences within markets and even within individual stores. The result is that when you shop at 7 Eleven in Queens, New York, you'll likely be shopping a very different range of products than what you'd find in Bartlett, Illinois. By choosing remarkable locations, but then doing the extra work of tailoring assortments to local needs, the 7-Eleven model becomes tough for competitors to replicate.

5. OFFER REMARKABLE PRICE WITH DIFFERENTIATED PRODUCTS, SERVICE OR EASE OF ACCESS You're driving along and discover that you're almost out of gas. You arrive at an intersection with two gas stations. One offers regular gas for a slightly lower price than the other. For the most part gas is gas. So, any rational person would choose the cheaper of the two, right? The answer is *maybe*. It depends on a number of other factors: the ease with which you can pull into the station without fighting traffic, the apparent cleanliness of each station and the other products and amenities each might offer. Perhaps you've had a bad service experience at one before. All of these things are considered against the savings.

Price, of course, has never been an absolute measure, but rather a modifier of value. If something breaks after the first use, does it matter that you paid less for it? If you spend an hour on the road to save a few dollars at a discount store, are you really saving anything? If you have to put up with rude and belligerent staff to save a buck or two, does it still constitute better value? On its own, price is not a competitive position.

There may be no better case to exemplify this need to compete beyond price than that of Walmart. For most of the company's history, its go-to-market position was predicated on price dominance, while it differentiated itself on convenience, given the level of in-store product assortment. There was very little in the way of proprietary products, and service was largely nonexistent, but it carried a boatload of product, and claimed to sell it for less.

Unfortunately for Walmart, the competition—and particularly the Internet—caught up to it on product selection. This left Walmart in a dogfight with dollar stores that had become adept at plumbing the depths of price on like items, and companies like Amazon that had in many ways become the biggest of all big-boxes, selling an assortment of biblical proportions with sharp pricing, and shipping it like lightning. Meanwhile, players like Target were stepping up with unique, original product designs that only served to highlight just how commoditized and boring Walmart's selection was. In essence, Walmart lost its dual-threat capability, and it has struggled ever since.

Therefore, any brand that sets out to dominate its market on the basis of remarkably low pricing must also be prepared to differentiate itself on some other aspect of its business—be it product, service or ease of access—to be sustainable. Someone will always come along who is willing to sell what you sell for less, so there *has* to be more to your position than price alone.

―――――

CUSTOMER EXPERIENCE IS A RESULT, NOT A COMPETENCY

You may have noticed the conspicuous absence of any mention of *customer experience* as a competitive attribute. It might seem a strange omission given that many businesses operate under the belief that it's their primary advantage over competitors.

In truth, there may be no term more overused and amorphous as *customer experience*. I defy you to find a marketing conference that doesn't harp on its importance and extol its competitive virtues. This experience has become like a garnish that we slather liberally over every plan we hatch in retail, believing that it will make the plan somehow more attractive or relevant. As a result, companies across North America irresponsibly sink too many hours and dollars discussing, mapping, designing, redesigning, training and surveying "the customer experience." Yet despite all this, as a consumer, how many awesome (really awesome) experiences do you enjoy in an average week? One? Maybe two? None? Hell, you'd think we would be swept off our feet everywhere we shop with all the experiential work that's supposedly going on!

And how many retail executives can really and truly explain in a sentence what *their* customer experience is and how it's any different from the shop down the street? When you check into a Hilton hotel, is there a trademark difference in experience from the Marriott hotel a block over? When you rent a car from Hertz, is the experience more memorable than what you get at Budget? I've even heard retail executives say that despite being almost identical to a competitor in every respect, they provide a better overall customer experience.

I wonder how this can be when, if your product, pricing, service and ease-of-access factors are identical to a competitor's, you have little ability to create anything more than the *identical customer experience* to your competitors.

If we're being honest, for most retailers the notion of customer experience has become an empty catch phrase that very few brands can truly articulate in lucid terms, much less animate.

There's a disconnect because most retailers feel that customer experience is something that gets engineered at an executive off-site meeting, and then handed to staff in a memo for execution. Many treat it as something that resides outside of, or in addition to, their product, pricing, service and ease of access—they feel that the experience is something peripheral to these core elements.

In reality, customer experience is merely the external expression of every internal decision that a brand makes. It is not one big idea, but rather a million moments of truth that are inextricable from the fabric of the brand.

So, if we're serious about customer experience, then we must first agree on what a brand is.

The question "What is a brand?" has been debated ad nauseam. *Brand* is a noun that some argue can only be a verb if you're marking cattle. Others maintain that a brand is logos, font styles and other trademarked elements. Some brands are companies, while other brands are merely the property of companies. Some feel that no one but the consumer *really* owns the brand, while other brands clearly feel that they own the consumer.

SO, WHAT IS A BRAND?

Beliefs, Customs and Artifacts

The simplest and most profound definition for *brand* that I have ever heard was shared with me by Thomas, a wonderfully brilliant, and frequently misunderstood, boss I once had.

Thomas maintained that at its essence, a brand was nothing more or less than a *culture*—a distinct way of being that is shared by a group of like-minded people. He maintained that the two things—brand and culture—did not exist independently of one another, but were in fact one and the same thing. Thus, if you have remarkable culture, you should possess a remarkable brand. And vice versa. If the culture sucks, the brand will likely suck too.

I couldn't help but agree with Thomas, but it prompted me to wonder: If a brand is indeed a culture, then what is a culture?

If you look at it in anthropological terms, a culture is generally found to be any group—or tribe, if you will—that shares three fundamental things: *beliefs*, *customs* and *artifacts*.

Beliefs are the guiding precepts of the tribe, the underlying motivation for all activity. *Customs* are the unique ways in which day-to-day activities of the tribe are carried out. And *artifacts* are the physical items associated with the tribe—tools, trinkets, clothing, furnishings, homes, etc.

Imagine that 10,000 years after the end of human existence, aliens arrive on earth and begin digging around. They would undoubtedly uncover evidence of our earthly beliefs—religion, politics, law, etc. They would also surely find evidence of customs such as marriage ceremonies, court proceedings, elections and sports. And, finally, they would discover countless artifacts of daily life on earth, including cars, furniture, buildings, jewelry and clothing. It stands to reason that all of these things, when put together, would give these aliens important clues about the human species and who we were as a culture. These things would be all the aliens would need to define our culture and reconstruct our story.

A brand is no different. The beliefs, customs and artifacts of your brand are ultimately what define it, and they culminate in this thing that we refer to as *customer experience*. Like Russian dolls, the elements of beliefs, customs and artifacts nest neatly inside one another. No one element is any more or less important than the others.

BELIEFS   In his 2009 book *Start with Why*, author Simon Sinek points out that just about every company understands what it does. Some companies even understand how they do it. Far fewer companies, he argues, have any sense at all of *why* they do it. They don't have a firm grasp on the overarching idea, purpose or belief that propels them along as an organization or *tribe*.

Sinek is also quick to add that those companies that have a clear sense of *why* they do what they do tend to outperform their competition. He points to the example of Apple computers, which could have, like most computer companies, focused its message only on the technical aspects of its products: ram, gigs, pixels, etc. But it didn't. Instead, Apple believes in challenging the status quo and being fundamentally different from its competitors. This is the *why* at the core—so to speak—of Apple. This is what fuels the brand. The design of its products and the marketing and sales experiences cohere into an expression of that core belief.

Sinek also makes the point that the mere pursuit of profit won't cut it as the *why* behind your brand. Profit, he maintains, is an outcome—a result of one's work—and not a core belief. However, it is also true that brands with strong core beliefs do tend to be more profitable.

None of this is to say that you can't be successful by ripping someone else off or by trying to make a quick nickel—you can! It happens all the time across just about every product category. The problem is that it's rarely sustainable, especially with today's unprecedented speed of innovation. Pretenders and profiteers are no match for an army of people aligning themselves with a common and compelling belief. In fact, there may be nothing more powerful.

One of the finest current examples of a company with strong core beliefs is Chipotle Mexican Grill. From the instant you open its website, the belief system at the core of Chipotle's brand hits you with the intensity of a habanero pepper! Natural ingredients, family ownership and sustainable farming practices are the *why* at Chipotle. The company just happens to support this belief through the food it serves.

Scan this to watch Chipotle's much-lauded video, *Back to the Start*.

Consumers therefore aren't merely buying *what you do* or *how you do it.* They're also (and often most critically) buying *why you do it.* The organization's intrinsic belief is what drives a sense of community and affiliation in its customers.

This clarity of belief is equally effective at identifying great staff—staff who share a deep sense of belonging to the brand. As Sinek points out, "If you hire people just because they can do a job, they'll work for your money. But if you hire people who believe what you believe, they'll work for you with blood and sweat and tears."[4]

So, try this: Assemble your senior leaders and ask each of them to write down why the organization does what it does every day—beyond the motivation to make a profit. You will likely get a variety of responses, from the mundane to the more thoughtful. In some cases, you might not get any response at all. Then it's time to be concerned. Regardless, forge ahead to find your *why*. Without the why, you can't move to the next step. Frankly, without the why, the next step doesn't even matter.

CUSTOMS   Once you've gone through the often trying process of aligning the organization around a common and firmly held belief or purpose, you can then (and only then) begin to identify and design the *customs* that flow organically out of it. These become the unique ways that your brand goes about doing things, which are highly distinguishable from other brands. After all, what makes one brand discernibly different from another is never a hollow platitude scrawled somewhere in a company handbook that no one reads. Rather, it's the actions and behaviors of every member of the brand that set it apart every day. Brand customs include every nuance of how members of the company relate to consumers as well as to one another. Language and communication, dress, routines, methods and processes, standards and expectations, education and so on are all important customs. What's even more important is that these customs are unique, relevant and appreciated by your customers and employees. And, above all, it's vital that customs be congruent with the brand's core belief.

Since the death of Steve Jobs in 2011, the retail industry has learned more about the inspiration that drove much of how Apple ran its stores, which in most respects flew in the face of conventional retail thinking. This, of course, was because Apple strove NOT to be a typical retailer. The pared-down assortment, the gallery-style sales floor for customers to play in, the no-pressure help from staff, the mobile point of sale and payment, the Genius Bar, warranties—everything—stemmed from the powerful core purpose of challenging the status quo. Apple didn't just do things a little differently; it took a radical approach to defying retail industry paradigms and, in the process, established entirely new benchmarks for retailers everywhere.

In fact, the experience was so precisely engineered that there were even certain things that employees were not permitted to say while helping customers. For example, the word *unfortunately*, as in "Unfortunately, we don't have that item in stock," was never to be uttered. Instead, staff were instructed to use the words *as it turns out*, as in "As it turns out, we don't have that item in stock," which Apple viewed as a less negative way of communicating the same out-of-stock situation. From there, staff were instructed to offer a solution aimed at making the customer happy, despite the situation.

Similarly, staff were coached not to "sell," but rather to cheer customers up, reassure them, recommend solutions and ultimately help them, working on the assumption that happy people become buyers. None of these brand customs was an organic chance happening. Brand development and execution were remarkably deliberate, designed and aligned with the idea at the nucleus of the brand—*Think Different!*

Ironically, retailers attempting to replicate the Apple experience fail to realize that there's no one thing that defines it. It's not merely the merchandising, the training, the product, the stores, the Genius Bar or anything else. It's the totality—the gestalt of all of these unique customs that culminates in what we know as the Apple experience. It's as unique as a fingerprint. Attempting to replicate Apple is like a neighborhood in Texas pretending to be Queens, New York. The culture is simply too unique to be copied.

ARTIFACTS   Artifacts are the things you use to carry out the customs of the brand on a day-to-day basis. These include the products themselves, websites, signs, store designs, fixtures, clothing and equipment—every single thing the business uses to perform. If you thought getting to this point meant the hard work was over, I've got bad news: this is the toughest part. Because each of these things, regardless of how seemingly small and inconsequential, is in fact a critical brand decision that speaks volumes about who you are as a brand. The really tiny stuff can make or break you.

The vice-chairman of Ogilvy Group UK, Rory Sutherland, gave a brilliant TED Talk entitled "Sweat the Small Stuff," in which he describes the disproportionately huge impact that small gestures have on a customer's experience.[5] This, he explains, runs contrary to how most organizations allocate time, effort and money. Most spend vast amounts of resources trying to impress customers with the big stuff, when, in fact, it's the little things that are often the most memorable.

He shares a great example of the salt and pepper pots that one finds on a Virgin Atlantic Upper Class flight, which, as Sutherland says, are so unique and fantastically designed that the first thought for most passengers is how they can get away with stealing them! The punch line is that inscribed on the bottom of the pots are the words "Pinched from Virgin Atlantic Upper Class." That's right—you're invited to steal them!

It would be easy for most companies to overlook what seems like such a small thing. Likewise, I'm certain that there must have been dozens of large-scale customer-facing projects that would have seemed to warrant priority over salt and pepper pots. But someone at Virgin did make these a priority and also chose to make them remarkable, and it wasn't all for naught. These wonderful little brand artifacts were cited by many Virgin Atlantic passengers as one of the most memorable aspects of their entire Upper Class flight.

Scan this to watch Rory Sutherland give his TED Talk, "Sweat the Small Stuff."

EVERY LITTLE THING YOU DO IS MAGIC

Every little thing, in the end, is a significant moment of truth for the brand and a vital part of the customer experience. Therefore, brands that deliver the most powerful customer experiences are also those that have the most clear and articulated beliefs, the most unique and well-developed customs and the best-designed artifacts. Brands like Apple, Whole Foods Market, Starbucks, Virgin, Amazon and others deliver the most powerful brand experiences because they are, in essence, the most fully personified brands in their categories. They simply act, communicate and socialize more like civilizations than corporate structures.

There's one other thing that brands like these share, and it may be the most important thing of all.

They're all hated by someone.

In fact, each one of these brands has, at some point, been attacked, singled out, keelhauled or burned in effigy by analysts, the press, Wall Street, bloggers or consumers themselves. They're just not everyone's cup of tea. And that is precisely why they've been so successful. They don't want to be everyone's cup of anything!

In what is a great article in *Fast Company* entitled "Why Your Brand Should Piss Someone Off," marketer Austin McGhie makes this point: "Apple. Mercedes. Virgin. Red Bull. Fox News. W Hotels. Snooki and Kim Kardashian. Every strong and focused brand, just like every strong and focused person, creates this love/hate dynamic to some degree." In other words, if no one hates you, chances are no one loves you much, either—you're not worth being passionate about, one way or the other.

This consumer passion of course requires one of two things on the part of leadership: either a maniacal, obsessive and over-the-top level of single-mindedness, or simply the organizational courage to let certain potential customers walk away. Leaders like Lululemon's Chip Wilson, Apple's Steve Jobs, Starbucks's Howard Schultz and many others have all, at one time or another, been labeled as obsessive and even eccentric in their unrelenting focus and often controversial stances. These leaders, like their brands, are polarizing and far from average. Creating a strong culture ultimately means having the confidence to risk alienating some consumers, your boss and, yes, even the board in defense of the brand as a whole!

McGhie perhaps sums it up best saying, "It's like life: the only way to have everyone like you is to avoid taking a controversial stance on anything. If you are willing to be anything to anybody—to surrender your identity and your individuality— no one will have strong feelings about you either way. You won't stand out to anyone and you won't offend anyone. You simply won't matter. Is that the fate you want?"

Maintaining market leadership will also require that significant risks be taken. When Starbucks launched VIA, its line of instant coffee, it ran a substantial risk of alienating those customers who associate Starbucks with gourmet, crafted coffees only. And yet, to bolster its business, particularly in the UK and Asia, it accepted the risk.

In the mid-2000s, faced with unrelenting competitive pressure from Walmart, Target disengaged from head-to-head competition and adopted a cheap-chic approach to its marketing position, despite the clear and present risk of losing bottom-feeding price shoppers. The risk proved an unqualified success.

Apple makes at least one product obsolete each year with the launch of a new, upgraded version, constantly risking the disenfranchisement of those who now own the outdated model.

Not all these risks pay off equally, and for some, like JCPenney and their pricing structure, the jury is still out. As hard as Ron Johnson is trying to shift to a new model of pricing, free of silly promotions and pseudo-discounts consumers, analysts and shareholders are pushing back. Creating change—even for a former Apple shining star like Johnson isn't easy.

One thing, however, is certain: in the new age of consumerism that we're embarking on, there's no room for cowards. The new law of average dictates that any brand that willfully chooses to ride the centerline of mediocrity will be road kill.

Remaining safe from the tyranny of an ever-expanding middle means constantly changing, tweaking, risking and evolving. It means making distinct, definitive and often unpopular choices without bowing to pressure from competitors, boards and, most of all, customers. It means going all in.

In short, it comes down to this: you need to figure out what your brand is really all about and why it's truly remarkable. You need to identify the galvanizing belief that burns at its heart. You need to articulate the customs and rituals that make it unique and give it soul, as well as the distinct artifacts that lend it identity and bring it to life. You need to zero in on the one thing that you do better than competitors, and you need to do it every minute of every day.

6

Who Owns Your Brand?

THERE'S A COMMERCIAL that has been running on TV as I have been writing this book. You might have seen it. It's for a product called 5-hour Energy, which is a two-ounce shot of liquid formulated to deliver what amounts to a temporary metabolic defibrillation and burst of wakeful consciousness—part of a balanced diet if you're a college student or truck driver. The brand was introduced to the market in 2004 and led a wave of other similar energy-shot brands. The effects of these energy shots have been widely debated, and because they're largely unregulated and not subject to rigorous government testing, the jury remains out on them.

Like most, I don't often listen intently to commercials. In fact, I record most of the shows I watch so that I can avoid commercials altogether. But there was something about this particular commercial that caught my attention.

If you haven't seen the ad, it features a very officious, credible-looking woman sitting on a desk beside a monstrous stack of papers—which we are led to believe are surveys. She confidently delivers the following dialogue:

> We asked over 3,000 doctors to review 5-hour Energy and what they said was amazing. Over 73 percent who reviewed 5-hour Energy said they would recommend a low-calorie energy supplement to their healthy patients who use energy supplements—73 percent!

While she's speaking, a series of fine-print disclaimers appear at the bottom of the screen. You'd need to have a magnifying glass handy to read them.

I ran the stats she quoted over in my head once or twice. There was something about them that harkened me back to my seventh-grade algebra class. The whole thing sounded oddly like a trick question that a teacher with a modicum of dark humor might put on an exam to submarine his or her students. Something about this claim of "73 percent" just didn't wash.

So, I did what any self-respecting consumer would do. I took the issue to the mighty oracle Google! And after a quick search of "5-hour Energy +3,000 doctors," I discovered that I was hardly the only one more than a little suspicious of the claim. In fact, there were literally hundreds of posts, queries and discussions from people who were every bit as dubious as I was.

What's more, some of the really smart ones out there had actually done the arithmetic. Here's what they discovered.

- The 73 percent of doctors surveyed **do not** recommend 5-hour Energy, but rather only a *low-calorie energy supplement*, of which 5-hour Energy happens to be one of many.
- These 2,190 doctors are not recommending low-calorie energy supplements for consumers in general, but rather

only for those (healthy) patients who *already use energy supplements*—which by definition would be a much smaller group.

- On close inspection, the fine print cagily admits the fact that of these 73 percent of doctors recommending low-cal supplements, *only 56 percent (1,226) actually recommended 5-hour Energy* based solely on reviewing the label and ingredients.

- More fine print then sheds dim light on the survey's method, which in this case was 500 online surveys and 2,500 in-person surveys, which it adds represent only *50 percent of those approached.* So, one has to wonder, what the heck happened to the other 50 percent of doctors (2,500) who were also approached? Why weren't their opinions included? What were the criteria for omitting their responses and keeping the others? Hmm?

- In actual fact, the sample group was not 3,000 doctors as the ad claims, but rather *5,500* doctors. The published results, however, were based on only 3,000 of these surveys, for reasons completely unknown to consumers.

Long story short, when you grind through all the math and fine print, at best only 1,226 of 5,500 (22 percent) of doctors could have possibly recommended 5-hour Energy (to their healthy patients who already use energy supplements) based on nothing more than a cursory review of the label and ingredients. Not 73 percent as the ad would have us believe.

Not exactly an overwhelmingly positive study by any standard. Yet, without understanding the truth behind these stats, it seemed like a slam dunk for 5-hour Energy.

Most incredible to me was that despite the hundreds and hundreds of blogs, discussions and social comments calling the brand out on what most felt was a grossly misleading ad, there was not one reply, rebuttal or response from the company. Not one.

I decided to see if 5-hour Energy had a YouTube channel—which it does. Among the videos posted there was the "3,000 doctors" commercial. I scrolled down to the comments section, eager to see what people had to say about the ad and how the brand was responding to them. It came as little shock to see that comments for that particular video had been disabled. The lights were on but no one was home.

Sensing a trend, I went over to Twitter to see what, if anything, consumers were saying about 5-hour Energy. I found that there was a steady stream of mentions of the product. They ran the gamut from those who appeared to absolutely love the product to those who, like me, had come across their misleading commercial and were a little irritated. Some said they hated the taste, some called it snake oil and others meanwhile swore by the drink's effectiveness. Some had even created their own high-octane wake-up recipes using 5-hour Energy. One would think that with such an engaged audience, the brand would be right there among its consumers, listening and responding to their comments, assessing what they felt and how the product could improve. Not the case at all.

As a matter of fact, amid all this rich chatter about the brand, I found one lonely and oddly tangential tweet from the brand itself. It said: "Hey #NASCAR fans! Have you entered the 5-hour ENERGY® Racing - Scavenger Hunt Contest yet?"

5-hour Energy had thousands of consumers talking about its brand (both positively and negatively) and the best it could muster was a passing promotional and hugely irrelevant tweet? What does this say about the relationship between the brand and the consumer?

To be fair, 5-hour Energy is certainly not the only brand disregarding the conversation around its product. If anything, it just makes a good poster child for the extraordinarily difficult time many brands are having in an environment inhabited by a new and decidedly more savvy and connected consumer. For brands like 5-hour Energy, though, it is akin to a self-inflicted wound. They're not tuning in to a new and important reality.

All around us brands are being made to atone for their errant actions, erroneous claims and unfortunate f-ups by empowered consumers armed with new tools to sniff out the truth and share it with others—many, many others. Whether it's Victoria's Secret getting called out for being wasteful and destroying returned merchandise, Nestlé being criticized for chopping down rain forests or Apple being made to answer for working conditions in China's Foxconn manufacturing site, brands are being called on the carpet by consumers with increasing alacrity. It doesn't seem to matter how deep brands bury the truth, there's someone in the world with the time, bandwidth and determination to dig it up and tell the world.

So, who really owns the brand? It's a question that marketers are struggling with every day.

Some vehemently suggest that we have entered an era where marketers, manufacturers and retail chains no longer *control* their own brands, but are merely stewards of the brand on the consumer's behalf. The collective conversation around a brand, they argue, has infinitely more influence and bearing on public perception than any message a marketer can dream up and push down the pipe.

Others, like *Six Pixels of Separation* author Mitch Joel, argue that the notion of consumer control over brands has become somewhat of a myth perpetuated by overly zealous social media fundamentalists. In a recent *Huffington Post* article, Joel wrote:

> As someone who spends the majority of his time in the boardrooms of some of the biggest brands in the world, please trust me when I tell you that the marketers are firmly in control of the brand...The brands control the brand. The consumers can (somewhat) influence the brand message. Brands still choose their products and services, they decide on the pricing, placement and promotion of the brand. They work (either internally or with an advertising agency) to set the tone, feeling and emotions that they want the brand to capture in the zeitgeist of the world.[1]

To Joel's point, things can go horribly awry when brands give too much latitude to their customers to define their message for them. Take the McDonald's #McDStories Twitter train wreck. During a simple little January 2012 campaign on Twitter called #MeetTheFarmers, intended to shine a positive light on the burger restaurant's focus on fresh produce, the company made the decision to append a tweet with the hashtag #McDStories. The audience took this as an open invitation to share their own McDonald's stories. What ensued was a torrent of negative, stomach-turning and sometimes frankly hilarious consumer tales of experiences with McDonald's food. The hashtag blew up so badly that the company had to quickly intervene to pull it down—the Twitter equivalent of riot control.

So, to relinquish control of your brand message to consumers without careful forethought and management is clearly not the answer. In fact, it's really just lazy marketing to expect consumers to fall all over themselves to *tell you why they love you* in such an artificial or staged way.

COLLECTIVE BRANDING

What we've embarked on is the age when both marketers and consumers collectively shape the conversation, community and public identity of a brand.

First, and without question, technology has given consumers an unprecedented level of control over their buying behaviors and decisions. In general, we have become tremendously more thoughtful about how and where we spend our money. And contrary to what some view as a temporary flight to frugality, studies indicate that these conscientious buying behaviors are far more permanently rooted than most marketers wish to acknowledge.

Second, the rise of social networks and user-generated media has given consumers astonishing levels of influence over the buying decisions of others. With one well-placed video, article or comment, shoppers have the potential to reach thousands—even millions—of other consumers to influence their beliefs about a product, brand or service.

Perhaps most importantly, we've seen that both of these conditions, at high enough levels of amplification, can indeed exert enormous influence on the actions and attitudes of a brand or retail chain. So, while they may not control a brand's decisions, consumers can certainly exert control over the outcomes. And all of this has been a reality for a remarkably short period of time.

Ultimately what this new level of consumer control and connectedness demands are three new and absolutely essential behaviors that all consumer-facing businesses will have to adopt if they intend to thrive. And it's no exaggeration to say that brands unable or unwilling to adapt to these new conditions simply don't have a hope of sustained success in the years to come.

These new organizational competencies are *honesty*, *illumination* and *immediacy*—exactly the same three things that the folks at 5-hour Energy flagrantly threw a middle finger to in its "3,000 doctors" campaign.

Honesty, illumination and immediacy, if embraced and mastered, will provide remarkable competitive advantages for those organizations that step up to the challenge that these three competencies represent.

HONESTY

About a year ago, I came across a statistic that said that consumers between the ages of 18 and 34 are more accepting of advertising as truthful than are 35 to 54 year olds. I have to admit that this seemed counterintuitive to me. I would have expected the opposite to be the case—that older consumers, less adept with technology and weaned on conventional advertising would be more trusting of most of what they read, heard and saw in the media. But the study claimed just the opposite, and the statistical gap was significant. Seeing this statistic, one might assume that older consumers (having been ripped off on more occasions) were simply more cynical than the more naive Gen Y consumers.

When you stop to think about it, though, this growing belief in advertising among young consumers makes perfect sense. I mean, my father grew up in a world where companies could dump PCBs into rivers for decades before the media caught on, and even then corporations had the power to keep a tight lid on the fallout. My children, however, live in a world where citizen videos of rats running rampant in a fast-food restaurant are uploaded to YouTube in mere minutes and quickly shared by millions of viewers, forcing a multi-billion-dollar restaurant chain to respond like lightning. I have lived to see the transition between both of these disparate realities. Big companies can now find themselves backed into nasty corners with blinding speed by a 10-year-old kid with a smartphone! You see, Gen Y consumers believe more advertising because advertising is, by necessity, becoming more truthful.

Tell the Truth authors Sue Unerman and Jonathan Salem Baskin maintain that this is no longer a debate about the ethics or morality of corporate truthfulness. Instead, they argue, honesty is simply no longer optional given consumers' access to information and their ability to instantly and widely share what they learn with others.

One problem that the authors acknowledge is that while the concept of truth is often cut and dried in our personal lives, it can become decidedly more muddied in a business setting, particularly when the stakes are high and the boss is screaming for more sales and shareholders are demanding higher returns. Adding to the complexity is that being dishonest doesn't always mean telling lies. In some cases, dishonesty involves taking a small sliver of the truth and portraying it as the whole truth. In other cases, it means taking a rather banal fact and exaggerating its value to make it seem truly outstanding. In still other instances, it's not what a brand *says* but rather what it *doesn't* say that constitutes dishonesty— refusing to talk about things that might negatively impact the brand, and sharing only the positives. All of these behaviors represent shades of dishonesty.

"It's discouraging to think how many people are shocked by honesty and how few by deceit."

—Noel Coward

The one truth that supersedes all others is this: consumers now hold, in the palms of their hands, all the connectivity and computing power they require to learn just about anything they care to know about you brand, your stores or your products—whether you want them to or not. No matter what you're trying to hide, someone will find you out.

If ever there was a harbinger of this new reality, it's something called *The Open Label Project*. The brainchild of Scott Kennedy, founder of Axcelis and BitStar, and David Ng, formerly of TomTom, *The Open Label Project* can best be described as a blend of Twitter, Wikipedia and *Consumer Reports*. The big idea at the heart of it is to provide a platform where crowd-sourced comments and ratings can be digitally appended to any product that carries a barcode, thus making the project the world's largest single source of consumer reference data for every product on earth. Simply scan a product's barcode with the smartphone-enabled app and you'll have the ability to see other users' ratings, reviews, recommendations and warnings about that product. Comments can range from price and quality issues all the way through to political and environmental concerns.

Users of Open Label will not only be able to access categorized user comments associated with products, they will also be able to add their own ratings and reviews by scanning the product's barcode and appending their comment. In other words, every label on every product could potentially become an endless whiteboard where consumers can post their approval or disapproval of a brand for any number of reasons!

And businesses that thought they could simply cheat the system by paying for favorable reviews are beginning to pay the price for their dishonesty. Online review site Yelp for example, recently began placing, what it's calling, a consumer alert notice on listings for businesses that had been caught posting fraudulent reviews. The notice reads:

> We caught someone red-handed trying to buy reviews for this business. We weren't fooled but wanted you to know because buying reviews not only hurts consumers but also honest businesses who play by the rules. Check out the evidence here.

Yelp then provides a link to the offending reviews.

It all amounts to a new and (at least in the short term) awkward era where businesses will be forced to come clean about their culpabilities, weaknesses and deficiencies before consumers discover them for themselves. There will simply be no feasible alternative but to tell the truth—something that will no doubt strike fear into the hearts of many, many brands. In my opinion, though, this represents a stupendous opportunity where honesty will become as valuable a competitive advantage as great products, prices or service—an era where being truthful and open about your brand carries exceptional advantage. This, of course, begs the question: What do you do if in fact your products, stores or service levels aren't excellent? Maybe you're not even good! Can honesty help a brand that just plain sucks?

Well, it seems it can. Perhaps the most exemplary case study is that of the Domino's Pizza turnaround. In late 2009, in the face of falling sales, a debilitating viral YouTube video of employees doing gross stuff to food orders and swelling numbers of complaints about the quality of its pizza, Domino's made a daring decision. It would not only address consumer concerns about its products, but also actually go public in its response to the criticisms that were being leveled at it. Moreover, it would openly document its efforts to win customers back by reinventing its products! With that, the company produced a series of documentary-style videos showing Domino's employees discussing and expressing their feelings about consumer criticisms of their brand. They showed focus group footage of customers complaining about Domino's cardboard-like pizza crust and thin, tasteless sauce. They captured the efforts of staff intent on building a superior product through experimentation and trial. In short, they not only told but also *showed* customers that they had heard their complaints, that they cared and that they were intent on winning back their business.

The experiment had several positive results. Consumers were interested in trying the new Domino's pizza recipes, and they also developed empathy for an organization honest enough to admit its flaws and concerned enough to do something to remedy them. The company's sales reignited after the campaign, and despite a tough economy remain above industry average. Domino's could have hidden, but it chose not to. It could have simply issued a standard corporate statement but it took a risk in making itself vulnerable instead. Domino's was honest, it improved its product and it paid off.

It also takes enormous conviction to tell the truth when so many others in your category simply don't. It's easy to accept dishonesty as table stakes to compete. Such is the case in the grocery industry with respect to claims of locally grown, natural and organic products. In fact, many grocery chains are liberally throwing these terms around with questionable foundation.

UK grocer Booths is not one of these chains. With 29 stores across northwest England, Booths grocery store has battled successfully against behemoths like Tesco and Sainsbury's, and has done so throughout one of the most challenging economic periods in history. The company credits its focus on high-quality, locally sourced and naturally raised livestock and produce as the primary reason. The difference between Booths and other grocers making similar claims is quite simple. At Booths, the claims are true! In fact, the farmer that produces the supermarket's organically raised lamb is on a first-name basis with Booths's butchers. Those who work the fish counters at Booths know their supplier, Les, the shrimp man!

While many grocers ply their customers with lovely imagery of pastoral scenes and bushels of organic produce, waxing eloquent about their commitment to local producers, these same chains are often the ones beating these farmers down on price and out of business. In contrast, Booths makes a commitment to farmers to pay fair market price, plus a healthy premium—a commitment it keeps in each and every transaction. And in the larger scheme of things, the chain also supports a movement called Slow Food, a global lobby group staging resistance to the pervasive growth of big agribusinesses. When asked to sum up the Booths proposition, company head Edwin Booth says succinctly, "What I say to our marketing people is only sell what is real." This is not to say that Booths does not also sell imported items and non-organics; in the interest of offering appropriate variety and selection, it does, and it's honest about it.

Booths is one of a growing contingent of companies leveraging honesty as a key differentiator in their market.[2]

But coming clean isn't always easy, as JCPenney's CEO Ron Johnson would likely attest. Shortly after taking the helm of the ailing brand in 2011, Johnson elected to redesign the chain's pricing structure. The old structure was based on listing products at inflated prices, purely so that they could later be marked down for promotion. In essence, the consumer was simply paying the market price while being hoodwinked into thinking they'd gotten a great deal.

The strategy resulted in the chain staging a whopping 600 "sales" per year. Johnson attempted to do away with this, moving instead to a three-tiered pricing structure of everyday low prices combined with fewer but more honest promotions. No more nonsense.

If you think consumers would reward Johnson for his honesty, you're wrong. Sales plummeted, profits dropped and foot traffic in stores evaporated. Consumers whined about missing their coupons, shareholders whined about missing earnings forecasts and analysts called Johnson a lunatic. If that's not enough, many consumers, when surveyed, said they'd rather buy something on sale or with a coupon—even if they know the sale isn't genuine—than pay a regular price.

So, the path to honesty isn't always smooth or even rational.

Nonetheless, it's clear that for brands like Domino's, Booths and others, honesty has become a tremendously powerful and sustainable advantage. It's often a battle to implement and an even greater struggle to maintain when times are tough, but in a world of white lies, half-truths and omissions, honesty proves to capture consumer attention and win loyalty.

Yet so many other retailers and brands simply don't get it. Consider the number of companies everywhere you shop that tout customer satisfaction as their number one priority, yet consistently deliver horrible service with open indifference. How many manufacturers stand on quality and yet carelessly permit defects to go to market. How many retailers claim to have their customers' best interests at heart while trying to sell them high-interest credit cards? And how many organizations say their people are their greatest asset while treating them like indigent slave laborers.

For companies like this, the day of reckoning is just around the corner. If you make junk, your customers will know about it. If you place your own interests above your customers', they'll figure it out. And if your stores are run like sweatshops, someone—and you *have* to believe me on this—will take video of it. There's no more secret sauce, black box or project X. Consumers have computers in their pockets and they're getting to know how to use them! If your business depends on half-truths, fine print and carefully chosen omissions to survive, your days are numbered.

Does Honesty Mean Transparency?

But does all this honesty equate, as some suggest, to the need for radical transparency? Do consumers really want unrestricted visibility into every thought, feeling and organizational motivation? I'm not convinced they do. As a matter of fact, I think that to assume so can lead a brand into some pretty freaky situations. Recently there have been several examples where brands have shared information that, in my opinion, their customers really didn't need or necessarily want . to know.

For instance, in a recent interview, Chick-fil-A president Dan Cathy expressed what many viewed as being Chick-fil-A's organizational position on same-sex marriage. He stated, "We are very much supportive of the family—the biblical definition of the family unit. We are a family-owned business, a family-led business, and we are married to our first wives. We give God thanks for that."[3] As one might expect, protests, vitriol and even boycotts of Chick-fil-A ensued. Some U.S. cities and campuses went so far as to bar Chick-fil-A restaurants from opening within their confines. It got ugly.

Some might argue that any press is good press and that, after all, brands are supposed to be polarizing and that it's better to be notorious than forgotten right? I disagree. Regardless of where you stand on gay marriage, any reasonable person would agree that there is a huge difference between positive press and divisive controversy. Good brands do polarize, yes, but they do so on the basis of what they sell and how they sell it, not on the politics or sexual orientation of the people they sell it to.

Gay rights advocates protest outside a Chick-fil-A restaurant.
(AP Photo/David Tulis)

It's true that great brands take a very distinct position on the
way they go to market. And yes, they may exclude certain consumers as a consequence, but they do so on the basis of the customer's product tastes, preferences and levels of engagement
with what the brands sell—and the last time I checked, Chick-
fil-A made chicken sandwiches, not wedding arrangements. So,
the question is, what did Cathy and Chick-fil-A gain from this
whole incident, apart from the sheer joy of self-expression? Did
he enhance the chicken sandwich–eating experience for his
customers? Did he make his restaurants cleaner, brighter and
more enjoyable? And how much time, money and resources
went into damage control for his organization that might have
been directed toward making a better product, rewarding high-
performing franchisees or supporting charitable efforts?

In a similar sort of situation, much-admired yoga apparel
brand Lululemon recently printed shopping bags that carried

the cryptic question "Who is John Galt?" The name was a reference to the opening line of the book *Atlas Shrugged* by Ayn Rand, a tome that speaks to the virtues of a free-market philosophy and promotes the merits of individuals living to further their own self-interests. The book has become somewhat synonymous with libertarian thinking.

Customers, even loyal ones, who didn't understand the John Galt reference, were left thoroughly baffled. *What does this have to do with the pricey yoga pants I just bought?* they asked. Some of those who understood the political innuendo of *Atlas Shrugged* were even outraged. *How dare Lululemon make its customers tote around thinly veiled political references!* And others didn't really give it much thought at all. *Who's John Who?* they yawned, completely uninterested.

As was later revealed after much reporting, *Atlas Shrugged* happened to be very central to the personal and professional philosophy of Lululemon's founder Chip Wilson. The company used its blog to respond to the controversy, saying, "Our bags are visual reminders for ourselves to live a life we love and conquer the epidemic of mediocrity. We all have a John Galt inside of us, cheering us on. How are we going to live lives we love?"[4]

This is certainly not as inflammatory a message as many had assumed, and so it prompts one to wonder, if this was indeed the sentiment Lululemon was shooting for, wasn't there a more straightforward, decipherable and honest means of stating it? Why cryptic messages on shopping bags? Why confuse? Why alienate? Why not just say what you mean?

Purpose versus Politics

Given increasing organizational openness, coupled with a turbulent political and economic climate, it's worth wondering if we're likely to see much more of this sort of entrepreneurial self-expression. It's difficult to say for sure. What *is* clear is that consumers perceive a significant difference between those organizations they regard as purpose driven and those that use their business as a bully pulpit for political expression.

Purpose-driven CEOs like Zappos.com's Tony Hsieh, who happens to support the growth of small businesses in Zappos's home city of Las Vegas, may not please all consumers with their choice of purpose. However, leaders like Hsieh also aren't likely to deeply offend many consumers with their choices, either.

Using a brand as a grandstand for politics, on the other hand, rarely does anything but alienate, confuse and disenchant.

And for those brands that truly do believe that consumers want them to be their moral compass and political beacon, they may be well advised to have a look at a recent study by the Corporate Executive Board (CEB). The CEB surveyed over 7,000 people and found that what consumers want above all is for brands to help in simplifying their decisions about the products and services they need—and really nothing else. They just want brands to make their path to purchase less complex and onerous.

Please don't take this to mean that brands shouldn't also set out to build communities of interest in their categories for their most highly engaged followers. I believe that brands should absolutely seek to forge an emotional connection with their customers. There's ample evidence to suggest that consumers who join a brand's community online are significantly more inclined to buy and spend more when they do. But again, the most successful of these branded communities are those that bring people of different backgrounds and beliefs together to share their love of what you sell—not what your CEO thinks about politics or religion.

So, before they dive into the fishbowl, it's vital that brands keep in mind that, first and foremost, consumers depend on them to sift, sort and simplify their choices and make their lives less complex, without a lot of drama. Being honest as a brand is the first important step toward achieving this.

ILLUMINATION

It's entirely possible for consumers to discover and understand more about a product than even the people working in the factory that manufactures it do. Simply downloading an app like GoodGuide can imbue shoppers with the power to instantly determine if a product meets their unique and specific guidelines for health, environment and social impact—regardless of how many 10-syllable additives the manufacturer uses. Using tools like RedLaser, ShopSavvy, Google Shopper or any number of others, they can review, compare and get key pieces of unbiased information about products in almost any category. On sites like eBay or Etsy they can even find out how many times a seller has screwed over his or her buyers, or conversely, wowed them with outstanding service—all courtesy of eBay's buyer/seller feedback system!

One inevitable consequence of this new level of consumer empowerment is the phenomenon of *showrooming*—that is, customers visiting a physical store to check out products, only to order those same products from an online competitor, sometimes while they're still in the store! Several prominent retailers, including Best Buy and Walmart, suggest that they are being increasingly victimized by the likes of Amazon and other online retailers, who, by virtue of their low-cost online model, can undercut on price while stealthily getting to consumers via their mobile devices.

There's one huge problem with this line of thinking, however. It's not grounded in fact. Studies, like one performed recently by Kantar Retail, actually show that, on average, Amazon's prices are up to 20 percent *higher* than Walmart's! And that's before any potential shipping charges.[5] Another similar study by Barclays shows that Best Buy's before-tax prices are a mere 4.2 percent higher than Amazon's—hardly what one might regard as clear and certain price dominance.[6]

The wake-up call for all retailers is that consumers are not going to Amazon purely for low prices. Price has simply become the convenient scapegoat for the sore losers in Amazon's wake. Consumers are also not going there purely for information about products. They could gather that on their own. In fact, survey after survey confirms that shoppers turn to Amazon first and foremost for illumination—for the very specific way that Amazon combines extraordinarily detailed descriptions, user reviews (positive and negative) and item popularity ratings, and does so in a way that makes shopping easier and less complex.

By contrast, when we visit most stores we get scant, heavily biased and brand-generated information only, which does nothing to really illuminate our path to purchase. The reflex for most retailers of course is to promote only the positive and to insulate the customer from outside influence. The psychology of peer reviews is quite fascinating, though. In fact, 67 percent of customers are more trusting of product reviews that include both positive and negative scores.[7] It makes sense then that we are likely to be more trusting in general of information that is balanced.

I suspect that this was the motivation behind the decision of Four Seasons Hotels and Resorts to integrate reviews of its hotels from TripAdvisor directly into its recently revamped website. While most reviews are largely positive—a credit to the chain's attention to service—there are also those that are not. Four Seasons has chosen to put the good, the bad and the ugly out there for the world to see. Who wouldn't trust a hotel with the courage to do that?

Information versus Illumination

It is important not to confuse the two concepts of information and illumination. My God, with so many of us processing up to 34 gigabytes or 100,500 words of data each day, we hardly need more information. But it's exactly because of this information overload that we so desperately depend on brands for illumination. We rely on them to cut through the bullshit and help us make the right choice.

To understand the difference, one need only compare Microsoft and Apple. Microsoft provides information on its products—lots and lots of information. The strength Apple brought, however, was its ability to illuminate the concept of computing in an entirely different way, making it approachable and accessible for those who may not consider themselves geeks. Apple introduced a new lexicon to the category, and instead of talking purely about ram, gigs and bytes, it spoke in terms of beauty, functionality, creativity and entertainment. It designed its stores in such a way as to clearly illuminate the differences between products and to allow customers to play, discover and learn. It reinvented its category by illuminating its product completely and in a way that had never been done before.

So, strictly speaking, one might argue that 5-hour Energy did provide all the *information* consumers required to piece together the claims of its study. If you dug long enough and deeply enough, it was all there. However, one could hardly say that the brand did anything to truly illuminate the public. In fact, one could argue just the opposite. These sorts of games and deceptions simply won't cut it anymore.

The Personal Path to Purchase

Ultimately, illumination goes beyond simply presenting consumers with features, benefits and points of view from other users. True illumination uses all available information to point customers toward the things that are uniquely suited to their needs and no one else's. Amazon calls the process "item-to-item collaborative filtering," which involves providing customers with recommendations that are based on past purchases, items on their digital wish list or other related data that is at the retailer's disposal. All of this information serves to shine an even brighter light on the consumer's decision path and instill tremendous confidence in the retailer. Amazon, for example, generates upwards of 30 percent of its sales based on these recommendations.

Now compare this to the four-by-six-inch display signage proclaiming a couple of general product features and a price, which is what you're likely to find by product displays in a Best Buy and most other stores. Instead of being illuminated by the results of collaborative filtering, the customer is faced with a lack of personalized service, or potentially utter confusion, while staring like a zombie at a wall of televisions in a department store, where only price markers differentiate the products from one another.

You can't compare the experiences, can you? The wicked reality that's eating Best Buy's lunch isn't the fact that Amazon is 4.2 percent sharper on price, but rather that it provides an infinitely better, less biased and more robust level of illumination than its competitors. It provides information that's personalized to each customer's needs and preferences and makes the buying process easier. Quite simply, online retailers that are illuminating the path to purchase are outgunning brick-and-mortar stores, and their prices (when they are indeed lower) are merely a bonus, only serving to solidify the decision in the consumer's mind.

Best Buy is not even remotely close to leveraging its physical stores, onsite products and displays and service staff to challenge Amazon's position. Best Buy hasn't done anything to connect the information and product reviews that it *does* have online with the stock in its stores. For Best Buy and others in the same boat, I can't help but wonder why not.

These organizations choose to fixate on the marginal Amazon price advantage, while missing a huge opportunity to use their physical store advantage and become the ultimate illuminator in the electronics category.

Whether you're a manufacturer or retailer, in a world where consumers have access to all the information they need, your job is no longer simply to provide more and more information. Rather, you must brightly illuminate consumers' paths to purchase by giving them the best information with which to make a sound decision based on their unique needs and preferences.

Tiffany & Co. sales staff for example have a brilliant ability to cut through the hundreds or thousands of jewelry items they offer in-store and zoom in on just the right item for a particular client. This isn't a matter of simply supplying the customer with loads of information or choice but rather illuminating their journey through the abundance of choice in a way that is distinctly pleasant and valuable. Thus, Tiffany and Co. further distance themselves from competitors—not by adding or augmenting but by editing their assortments and simplifying the purchase decision.

Radical Personalization

The future challenge for retailers, regardless of what they sell, is to not only create these sorts of powerful physical experiences, but also bring key aspects of online shopping to their in-store customers. It will soon become essential, for example, for all retailers to harness the technology that will allow them to recognize customers by name when they return to the store; access their past purchase history, wish lists and preferences instantly; and point them in a personalized way to the products that will delight them. They will need to incorporate the influence of shoppers' social graphs (their circle of friends on social networks) to show them which items their friends who shop there have enjoyed. They'll need to find ways to leverage location-based and check-in data to show shoppers the items that others in the store are currently focusing their interest on.

Various technology companies are rapidly homing in on these sorts of future capabilities to connect consumers' online and offline lives within the store environment.

For example, Facedeals is a facial recognition technology that uses cameras to recognize consumers based on their Facebook photos as they enter a business. It then presents the consumer with offers and recommendations that are customized based on their Facebook "like" history.

Along similar lines, European fashion retailer C&A, recently launched an incredibly ingenious project in their Brazilian stores whereby each time a particular item received a LIKE on the company's Facebook page, it was then tabulated and displayed on the in-store hangers used to display that item in their shops. Shoppers could then instantly gauge the general popularity of items while they shop.

Scan this to see how Facedeals works.

Mobile payment pioneer Square recently inked a deal with Starbucks in its development of a consumer application that, similar to Facedeals, automatically alerts staff to an individual's presence in the store through the company's Wi-Fi network. Although still in development, the app is expected to provide staff with key pieces of information related to the customer's preferences and loyalty dimensions. Square also indicates that this technology will allow customers to pay simply by virtue of facial recognition.

As these technologies evolve, they will allow retailers to illuminate the customer's path to purchase in a far more personalized and meaningful way, and provide consumers with completely unique experiences based on their individual needs, tastes and purchase histories. Illumination, as a competitive advantage, will mean delivering engaging, personalized and fully enlightening store experiences that are simply beyond compare.

IMMEDIACY

The promise of social networks for businesses was that, after almost 100 years of cold and impersonal mass media, marketers, store operators and even C-level executives would have the opportunity to do what they had desperately been longing to do: connect directly, in a human way, with consumers in real time! Finally, they could discover what their customers really felt about their brand, products and services. They could win them over with instantaneous personalized responses to their queries, quandaries and complaints. In short, they could relate to their customers like people, not like markets.

In spite of this apparent zeal, today 76 percent of consumers who complain on Twitter receive no response from the company they've called out. No response of any kind.[8] Furthermore, companies on average only respond to 5 percent of all questions posted to branded Facebook walls.[9] In fact, over half of consumer-facing *Fortune* 500 companies don't even provide links to their Twitter profile or Facebook page on the contact page of their website.[10]

So, why the disconnect? If brands want so badly to connect with customers, why do so few of them seem even mildly interested in seizing the opportunity? Why are many running in the opposite direction? What gives?

It's true that social media offers what every marketer seeks—instant and genuine engagement with their audience. But here's the dirty little truth that no one likes to admit: it's exactly this new level of intimacy with the audience that marketers fear like the plague. Most don't really want interaction with their consumers at all.

Live versus Studio Retailing

The brilliant Canadian classical pianist Glenn Gould was notoriously terrified of performing in public. By age 32, he had retired from performing in public altogether, choosing instead to perform only on radio for studio recordings. He was once quoted as saying, "I detest audiences. I think they are a force of evil."

Of course, Gould was far from being the only artist who suffered this fear of live performance. Barbra Streisand, Sir Laurence Olivier, Andrea Bocelli and even Lady Gaga all experienced what were sometimes paralyzing bouts of stage fright.

In contrast to the stage, a studio is controlled, detached and safe, and for many artists it is the preferred performance space. It allows one to redo, rework and perfect before packaging up work and sending it out to the public. It allows for good days and bad days without anyone knowing. And, above all, it is free of any immediate reaction from the audience—no standing ovations received perhaps, but no rotten tomatoes thrown, either.

This is quite similar to the reality that retailers face today. Most have become accustomed to doing their work behind the scenes—organizing agency meetings, orchestrating focus groups, planning market tests, executing ad runs and the like— all from the relative safety of their studio. Most are simply not attuned to real-time interaction with consumers. Others are simply not cut out for it.

To take a studio performer and throw him or her onstage can of course be a disaster. Yet, surprisingly, it seems like we expect marketers and store operators to easily make the transition over to this new level of immediacy and audience engagement.[11]

The fact is that it requires an entirely new skill set and temperament. Where the job of the retail executive before, say, 2004, used to be to methodically target markets, systematically develop clandestine plans and then boldly execute initiatives accordingly, the role is evolving now to be more creative, iterative, flexible and collaborative. The new marketer puts themselves in the scrum of consumers, listens intently, brings product and service solutions to their customer communities and then faces the reaction online and in store and in real time, adjusting quickly all the while.

This new level of immediacy also requires organizations to be more responsive and comfortable with ambiguity. In 1982, if the company president took two days to respond to a customer's letter, it was stellar turnaround. If the company takes two days to respond to a customer's Twitter rant, it is a failure of biblical proportions. This means that brands are being required to think much faster and respond sooner, and live with the imperfections that this level of responsiveness brings. The best organizations tend to spread the responsibility for customer interaction across the ranks, often to their highest levels.

For example, in July 2011, a Chipotle customer, writer (and non-pig-eater) Seth Porges (@Sethporges), discovered that the restaurant's pinto beans, which he had been ordering regularly, were cooked with pork. So he did as customers are increasingly wont to do: he summoned the gods of Twitter, expressing his shock that after ordering pinto beans on his burritos for years, he was only now informed of the porcine particulars of the recipe!

What happened next is interesting. Porges did not receive a letter. He wasn't sent a gift card. There was no apologetic e-mail from some customer-service underling. Nope. Instead, within minutes, he received a personal phone call from Chipotle's founder and CEO Steve Ells, who not only apologized for the problem but also promised to change the menu to clearly reflect the pork ingredients—which he indeed did. All this prompted Porges to head to Twitter once more, this time tweeting, "Just spoke to head of Chipotle. Said I got them to change menus to say Pinto has bacon! Awesome & nimble response! Thanks @chipotlemedia." Steve Ells's willingness to personally respond to this customer demonstrated three key things: 1) he practices courageous leadership; 2) he recognizes that Twitter and other social media sites are communication platforms first and marketing platforms second; and 3) he has a clear understanding that simply leaving a writer with thousands of Twitter followers to rant unabated on a social network isn't cool. Ells's immediacy that day solved the problem, and his response became a thing of legend in social media circles.

But it doesn't necessarily take the organization's fearless leader to make the difference. In November 2011, Virgin Atlantic made an upgrade to its reservation system. Unfortunately, the upgrade messed up certain reservations, affecting several thousand customers, who, as one might expect, began talking up their frustration on Facebook and Twitter. Where the brand could have done what most brands do—issue a blanket apology or press release—Virgin chose not to. Instead, members of the organization sent 12,000 personalized apologies via the same social media channels that they were received in.

Today, Virgin Atlantic and Chipotle's actions are still remarkable, given where most retailers are with respect to personal customer engagement. In a decade or two, however, this level of immediacy will be standard practice for any brand worth doing business with.

BRINGING IT ALL HOME

So, do consumers control your brand? Nope. Do they have unprecedented power to destroy it? Yup.

Brands that win in the new and incredible era of consumerism that we're entering will be those that have the courage to be honest about their products and services, the power to completely illuminate their customers' path to purchase and the balls to respond to consumers with complete immediacy. And all of this must happen regardless of the channel the customer chooses—online, in store, mobile or otherwise.

5-hour Energy respected none of these new tenets. The company wasn't honest and did nothing to illuminate the consumer's path with respect to its product. To top it all off, 5-hour Energy showed a complete lack of immediacy and responsiveness on any level. The organization failed my litmus test for a "future-proof" business. It's only a matter of time before someone comes along to obliterate them.

I also recognize that, as businesses that have emerged from over 100 years of corporate half-truths, hyperbole and general aloofness on the part of companies, these notions of honesty, illumination and immediacy as key competitive advantages might be hard to fathom. For some businesses it will undoubtedly seem like an uncomfortable departure from business as usual. But here's the thing: this isn't a departure at all. It's a return to the way meaningful commerce was conducted for thousands of years, before being interrupted by the aberration we call mass marketing. None of this is new. It's simply the way retail was always intended to be. Honest.

7

Rehumanizing Retail

ALLOW ME TO INTRODUCE you to my apparel retail A-team! First meet *Tensator*. She's our store concierge, and she's absolutely brilliant. She is a quick study, fluent in multiple languages and dresses with impeccable taste at all times. She's got a dynamite attitude, too—always friendly, welcoming and helpful. She's virtually perfect.

Next meet *Baxter*. Baxter is the team's workhorse. He's super-trainable and does most of the manual in-store tasks, from stocking shelves to counting inventory to retrieving customer orders. Baxter never objects to increasing workloads and he never, ever makes mistakes. Show him how to do something once and he'll do it perfectly the first time and every time, 24/7.

Then there's *Hunch*. Hunch is the whiz kid of the team. He gets to know each and every customer individually, tracks their unique preferences and previous purchases and uses all the information to come up with just the right recommendations that suit customers to a T. He's a genius!

CognoVision is in charge of store analytics. She records customer traffic in real time, allowing for adjustments in merchandising to optimize sales. She even changes the messages of in-store signage in real time to best match the demographics of the shoppers who are standing in front of her, and tracks their eye movement for signs of engagement. She sorts, organizes and reports all this data to Baxter, who ensures that items in the store are merchandised accordingly.

Bodymetrics makes sure that the clothing that Hunch recommends fits every customer perfectly. He takes body measurements in an instant, creating a map of the entire body, and then recommends the perfect clothes every time!

Finally, there's *Scan & Go*. They're our checkout team. *Scan* lets customers itemize the things they're buying while they shop and order non-stock items for delivery. *Go* tallies it all up instantly and allows for payment in one easy step.

Together, the team members combine their superpowers to create amazing experiences for customers. And what's more, they never ask for raises, days off or performance appraisals. They don't get holiday parties, collective bargaining agreements or pensions. Best of all, they never utter a complaint about any of it. It's pretty sweet!

If my futuristic retail team strikes you as being a little far-fetched, think again. Everything I just described exists and is quite functional today.

Tensator is in fact a brand of virtual assistant that is in use in many airports and other businesses around the world. The assistant can be programmed to meet the content requirements of any business, in any language and with multiple greeter physical appearances. Tensator has the potential to take the virtual world by storm.

Baxter is a new breed of user-friendly, easily programmable robot that can, in mere minutes, be taught to do manual tasks with inordinate levels of accuracy. At $22,000 Baxter is a fraction of the cost of typical industrial robots, and is far more cost-effective and efficient than a human equivalent.[1] And Baxter is hardly alone. Researchers at Carnegie Mellon

University are experimenting with robotic technology in the university bookstore. The robot they use is called AndyVision, and it autonomously patrols the bookstore floor, scanning, photographing and inventorying all products as it goes, using advanced image recognition. It then creates an out-of-stock and out-of-place list for management, and a 3-D map of the store to help customers easily locate the products they're looking for.

Further up the supply chain, logistics companies like Quiet Logistics, whose customers include retailers like Zara, Gilt and Bonobos already employ a team of 75 robots that work alongside human staff in the company's Devens, Massachusetts, e-commerce fulfillment facility, picking and packing orders over 20 hours a day.

 Scan this to watch Baxter the robot in action.

Hunch is an algorithmic, artificial intelligence program developed at MIT that combines user-data inputs with machine learning capability to gather and assimilate everything it can about a user, and then provide him or her with incredibly accurate product and service recommendations based on a series of decision trees. The more data Hunch receives from unique users, the smarter and more capable of making accurate recommendations it becomes.

CognoVision is an anonymous facial recognition technology recently acquired by Intel that is able to identify key demographic information about shoppers before instantly serving up in-store advertising that would be most appropriate based on the customer's age and gender. The same software then tracks the shopper's eye movement to gauge the length of engagement with the marketing message being displayed. CognoVision also offers technology that heat-maps customer traffic flows through retail spaces in real time, which allows merchants to rework dead zones or move key products to high-flow areas.

Bodymetrics is a full-body scanner, similar to what you'd find in an airport security area. It scans a potential customer's body (no need to remove one's clothing) and maps body dimensions precisely to recommend the ideal product to fit the customer's body type. These scanners are currently installed in several retail locations across the United States, and are fitting customers into over 100 different brands of clothing. And this is just one of many fitting-room technologies that are being experimented with. As recently as 2011, retailers like the UK's Topshop have also been experimenting with augmented-reality mirrors, which allow customers to virtually try on clothes in the store before even getting to the fitting room.

Lastly, Scan & Go is an iPhone-based self-checkout app that Walmart is currently experimenting with. The app allows customers to pre-scan their entire order as they shop and pay for everything in one step before leaving. This is only one of many self-checkout platforms being tested by retailers globally.

Let me reemphasize that everything I'm describing is not in the far-flung future—it is right now.

The question, however, is: Do Baxter, Hunch, CognoVision and the rest of this team *really* realistically represent the retail service employees of the future? In a word, the answer is *yes*. Indeed, in many retail environments they will be the only "employees" required, and will without a doubt be more reliable, trustworthy and cost effective than any human counterparts could be. And while one might imagine consumers being recalcitrant in accepting this sort of dehumanization of their shopping experiences, research shows just the opposite. A recent survey conducted for NCR revealed that two out of three U.S. consumers surveyed want self-service options when shopping, and that nearly half of the U.S. shoppers under the age of 45 who were surveyed want stores to offer self-checkout.[2] Perhaps this is the underpinning rationale for

Walmart's recent move to install nearly 10,000 self-checkouts in their U.S. stores.

Another recent survey suggested that more than 70 percent of Europeans had either a fairly positive or very positive view of robotics.[3]

So if you're counting on a *Terminator*-like war between us and the machines that seek to control us, you might be disappointed. The relationship between consumers and machines appears to be developing swimmingly! But how exactly did it come to this? How did we humans lose so much of our value as part of the retail supply chain? And what does this entire situation mean to consumers as well as to the future prospects of living, breathing retail staff? What the hell happened?

Once again, in order to gain a sense of direction moving forward, we need to glance briefly in the rearview mirror to fully understand how exactly we got here in the first place.

THE DEHUMANIZING OF RETAIL

Review any retail sales training program written in the past 50 years and you'll almost certainly encounter multiple uses of the word *rapport*. Rapport, or the relationship and understanding between people that builds trust and confidence, has long been regarded as the most critical aspect of effective customer service. In order to properly assess and address the needs of the consumer, the salesperson has to be able to fundamentally relate to those needs, to understand the customer's world. Then, and only then, the theory asserts, can salespeople recommend the best product, from personal experience, to satisfy the customer's needs with credibility. In other words, the more alike the realities of the customer and the sales associate are, the easier it is to build this essential rapport.

However, we know that the economic distance between the lowest-paid Americans (many of whom have been frontline retail workers) and the highest paid has widened dramatically over the last 30 years, and continues to expand at an alarming rate. How can a retail associate earning a mere fraction of what their customer earns, ever hope to develop genuine rapport?

It wasn't always like this though. In the 1970s, retail sales was a dignified and worthy profession that allowed people to support their families, buy homes and put kids through school. But wages became systematically stagnated, and retail, to an increasing extent, became the trade of the working poor. It was a job better suited to students, or, as it became for many, a job you took until you could find "real" work.

Today, the Federal Minimum Wage stands at $7.25—a significant rise from where it stood since 1997. Nonetheless, experts agree that this figure is desperately out of sync with inflation. If properly indexed to the corresponding increase in the cost of living, the minimum wage should be over $10. Despite the rather obvious math, roughly half of the nation's frontline retail workers today earn a little over $9.00 per hour. So how can a retail sales associate achieve rapport with a consumer who may be spending more on a pair of pants than the sales associate will gross from two full days of work?

The painful truth is that retail sales associates of today, who earn a national median hourly wage of less than $10.00 per hour, are more distanced from their customer (from a socio-economic standpoint) than they have been in more than 100 years. This makes even the remotest level of rapport between associates and their customers all but impossible.

And this wasn't the result of some isolated accident or mishap of economic policy. It was the product of a systematic, industry-wide decoupling of human beings from the retail equation in an effort to reduce costs. Throughout the 1980s and 1990s, companies clamored to embrace new technologies that promised to boost productivity, reduce costs and arrest growing retail losses—the majority of which were the result of escalating levels of employee theft. New inventory systems, point-of-sale technology and loss-prevention systems were installed to correct these problems and leave salespeople to focus on selling. Ironically, it was often these very systems that turned salespeople into mere slaves to the machine, unable to override system protocols and processes in situations that would have previously been easily sorted out with common sense and communication. Ironically, the very technologies that promised greater customer-centricity often ended up being the very things that conspired against it.

"Give me a stock clerk with a goal and I'll give you a man who will make history. Give me a man with no goals and I'll give you a stock clerk."

—*J.C. Penney*

To make matters worse, many of the middle-management roles within retail companies were being eliminated as digital technology became more pervasive. In many organizations, the roles of area, district and regional managers became redundant because more and more of the day-to-day data collection, analysis and reporting was being systematized. Other middle-management functions like store merchandising and training were increasingly being outsourced to third-party providers to lower operating expenses and head counts. In many retail chains, this all but eliminated the possibility of upward mobility, which might have allowed the aspiring frontline retail employee to ascend the corporate ladder and one day reach the boardroom. The ladder was simply missing too many middle rungs, and consequently frontline sales became a low-paying cul-de-sac—a road to nowhere. A stagnant minimum wage, combined with diminishing autonomy, mastery of work, employer trust and career mobility, further disenfranchised retail workers, and made them feel commoditized. The net effect was a deadly downward spiral in consumer experience. Service in many companies became (and remains) simply abominable. This, of course, only exacerbated the devaluation of retail sales-people and heightened companies' motivation to employ technologies to replace them.

And so it went; the more employees became disenfranchised, the lower their performance became. The lower their performance became, the harder companies worked to marginalize them. Increasingly, the sales associate became not much more than a glaring number on the profit-and-loss statement—a number most organizations felt an enormous compunction to shrink.

By the early 2000s, even retailers like Home Depot—which had long hung its hard hat on unrivaled customer service—began aggressively culling their front ranks. When Bob Nardelli took over Home Depot in 2000, he reduced overall staff levels and converted many full-time jobs to part-time. The chain that customers depended on for superior home improvement expertise had become a hollow box with hardly a sales associate to be found. And those who could be tracked down often weren't experienced enough to help.[4]

Regrettably, Home Depot wasn't the only one sacrificing its front lines. Between 1998 and 2008, after projecting a potential *gain* of hundreds of thousands of retail jobs, the Bureau of Labor Statistics reported that, in fact, there was a net decrease of over 92,000 retail workers nationwide. Despite rampant economic growth, the value, utility and presence of retail workers appeared to be shrinking at an astonishing rate.

Experienced, better-paid employees were being steadily shown the door in favor of cheaper, low-skilled workers who, instead of delivering personal service, were now largely responsible for shuffling product around the store and maintaining inventory systems and abiding by stringent operating protocols. Experience-makers were replaced with rule-followers.

Even the title of "salesperson" became largely removed from the lexicon of most retail companies, which opted instead for the less descript and vastly more ineffectual "store associate" moniker. If a brand ever had any real *salespeople*, they likely didn't work there anymore.

The eventual result was a retail world where humans began behaving more like machines, and machines began acting a little more like humans. The problem was that neither was very capable when it came to delighting customers. Inventory software was often completely inaccurate, self-serve systems were onerous and clunky and POS systems were frequently slow and prone to error. On the human side, employees were increasingly complacent, detached and in some cases downright belligerent. They were the victims of stagnating wages, low self-esteem and mind-numbing work.

Consumers found themselves trapped in a sort of purgatory, where store systems were inadequate to enable them to serve themselves and yet there were no salespeople available or even willing to serve them, either! Shopping routinely became like a horrid game of Marco Polo with customers roaming cavernous store aisles like the blind, while "store associates" scattered at the very sight of them. Except in this game everybody was a loser.

The retail industry had lost its soul.

―――――

You might think that's where the story ends―with the humanity of retail becoming a thing of the past, the value of human service decimated forever and the world as we know it coming to an end. Not so at all. In fact, I would argue just the opposite―that as our need for human service in retail situations diminishes, the *value* we place on extraordinary person-to-person experiences increases proportionately. That is to say, that as the world becomes more effectively self-service, the value of personal, human service will in fact escalate! Retail as an industry is "rehumanizing." And contrary to popular belief, the best days for those who work in retail and for consumers lie ahead.

What will soon be buried in the sands of time are the sorts of frustrating, disengaged and mediocre service experiences we still suffer, even today.

FULLY AUTOMATED VERSUS FULLY ANIMATED EXPERIENCES

There's been fervent debate surrounding the future strategic need for brick-and-mortar stores, with some arguing that given the stunning growth of online shopping, the horizon for physical stores is limited. I've seen nothing that would lead me to agree with this. I grant that as web, social and mobile commerce continue to grow, our dependency on brick-and-mortar retail purely as a form of distribution for products and services will steadily decline. We simply won't need stores in order to access the things we want and need. Online retailers like Amazon are already testing same-day delivery of products in select markets—a service that will be catastrophic for many middle-of-the-road retailers. So, I agree completely that the future will certainly see fewer stores.

But there are two things to keep in mind. First, at its core, shopping is a social activity. We shop not only to gather and acquire the things we need, but also to commune in public places, to be *with* people. I'll be the first to argue that online stores will get better and better at fulfilling the distribution aspect of shopping, but I would also hold that nothing will entirely replace the social experience of visiting the market. Second, although the list of things we as consumers are comfortable buying online grows each year, there are still things that are simply more confidently purchased in a physical store setting. My recommendation to brands, however, is not to focus so much on the *quantity* of stores that the market will eventually bear, but rather concentrate on the *quality* of stores that will be required to create unique value in a world where Amazon is willing to ship one of anything, anywhere.

For those worthy brick-and-mortar retailers that do remain, there will unquestionably be a new and dramatically higher consumer expectation that stores deliver experiences that are unique and remarkable—experiences that simply cannot be replicated digitally. The strategic future value of the store, therefore, will shift from distributing products and services to distributing remarkable experiences and favorable brand impressions. In essence, the store – once no more than a distribution point—will have to evolve into a dynamic media point, a place where the primary product sold is the brand itself. A living, breathing entity whose chief purpose is the creation and distribution of mind-blowing, jaw-dropping experiences. Experiences that drill a deep cognitive and emotional pipeline into the minds and hearts of customers. If the store is performing as it should, where the customer ends up buying (web, mobile, in-store) won't matter at all. They will have fallen, irreversibly in love with the brand and buying anywhere else would feel like cheating. Robin Lewis and Michael Dart, authors of *The New Rules of Retail*, put it aptly, saying: "A retailer or brand or service must first determine how to make its particular value offering so powerfully satisfying that it actually changes the consumer's brain chemistry—so mentally and emotionally compelling that at the mere mention of the brand or retailer or service, the consumer's brain releases a shot of dopamine, which triggers an instant desire to get or go to that brand."[5]

So, how exactly will retailers go about changing consumers' brains? I believe there can and will be only two distinctly different ways.

One is through the *fully automated* experience, which is largely guided by outstanding technologies that are supported almost invisibly by bright, highly trained humans. These will be amazingly seamless, pleasant and customizable experiences that allow consumers to walk away with the exact product they came for with ultra-convenience and ease. The objective of such stores will be to forge a deep *cognitive* association between the store and its ability to provide immediate satisfaction of the consumer's needs. By design, encounters with live staff in these stores will be rare and largely unnecessary. Systems, not people, will create the magic in these environments.

The other is a *fully animated* experience, where outstanding brand representatives are supported by advanced technology in delighting their customers. This is an entirely human, visceral and emotional experience, where consumers are guided through deep and enjoyable experiences with concierge levels of service. In these situations, the technology underpinning them is largely transparent to the consumer. Consumers in these spaces will forge an equally strong emotional connection between these stores and feelings of joy, high self-esteem and social connectedness. The potent combination of outstanding people and superb technology will work to enchant customers beyond their expectations.

There will be no viable in-between proposition. Anything that fails to achieve one or the other of these extremes will be largely overlooked as consumers seek out either the ultra-convenience of the automated environment or the deep fidelity of the animated environment.

It's important to clarify that neither of these experiences is inherently better or more valuable than the other—they will both have their place in the consumer's life. Furthermore, one shouldn't assume that fully animated experiences will always be confined to the sale of luxury goods. It's not always going to be that clear cut. It is safe to say, though, that in most situations where the retailer is setting out to achieve a high-fidelity position in its market, fully animated experiences will support it better, and likewise for high-convenience retailers, fully automated experiences are more likely to be appropriate.

What is nonnegotiable is that brands clearly articulate and align themselves on which experience they are designing, being careful to obey the new law of average—that all things average are invisible!

If you look around, there are now already faint signs of this experiential division taking place in the market. Within specific categories of goods, entirely different experiential approaches are emerging.

Brands like Gap, Old Navy, Banana Republic and Levi's are currently testing the full-body scanning technology described earlier in this chapter. The entire process is automated, resulting in customers receiving a personal shopping guide for jeans that allows them to almost instantly understand the brands, fit and finish that will best suit their body type. There is no need for human intervention here. No dependency on expert help. Here, the technology is quite obviously the hero.

By contrast, Nordstrom, renowned for personal service, has partnered with Joseph Abboud to provide its highly trained salespeople with an application that allows them to expertly assist customers in the design of made-to-measure suits. Over the course of 30 minutes, the salesperson and his or her customer work together closely through all aspects of style and material, as well as key measurements for a perfect fit. The one-of-a-kind suit is delivered to the customer within two weeks of order. Here technology is merely the enabler, while the salesperson steals the show.[6]

Signifying a similar experiential divide in the airline industry, Alaska Airlines and JetBlue are aggressively building out technology to ensure that the first employee that travelers need to speak to is the flight attendant on the plane. The goal is that check-in, baggage tagging and even boarding procedures all be completely self-service. These systems are currently being tested in several North American airports. By contrast, Delta Air Lines has partnered with Porsche to surprise and delight high-value frequent fliers with a high-speed ride from their landed aircraft to their connecting flight or parking space! Try getting that online! Neither of these experiences is necessarily better than the other. The point is that they're different and they're definitive.

Expect to see more of these sorts of experiential divisions within categories as brands are forced to choose which side of the automated or animated experience line they fall on. We should also anticipate that as technology in general evolves, the experiences at either end of the spectrum will only become more impressive, seamless and wow-inducing.

Retailers trapped in the middle position of yesteryear aiming to get by with mediocre systems and average employees will, to put it bluntly, be toast.

THE REHUMANIZATION OF RETAIL

So here we are, in a place where technology is quite capable of delivering profoundly wonderful experiences just about anywhere we happen to be, and consumers are more than capable of ferreting out their own information about a product or organization in a few clicks. At the same time, in some situations, consumers have heightened expectations of the overall retail experience and require exponentially better personal service than ever before!

So, how does this sort of cleaving of experiences impact the role and value of (human) retail employees? Does the industry need them at all, and, if so, what new skills, competencies and value must they bring in a future where mediocrity is extinct and consumer expectations are heightened?

What we will steadily witness is the replacement of low-skilled retail workers with two new and decidedly higher-caliber specialists: the retail technologist and the brand ambassador.

The Retail Technologist

Fully automated store experiences will hinge on seamlessly marrying a multiplicity of technologies to form one continuous and delightfully elegant experience for consumers. And as mentioned earlier, these experiences will have to be extraordinary and directly associated with ease, efficiency and immediate satisfaction.

The wizards behind the curtain will be people best described as "retail technologists," who are conversant with both the architecture of the experience and its desired cognitive effect on shoppers. They will have the technical conversancy and solid working knowledge of the various elements of web, mobile, location-based and in-store applications that tie the experience together. They will have a clear knowledge of marketing principles and executions, and be able to manage field maintenance and upgrades to stores as required. In essence, they will represent the former roles of regional marketer, systems specialist and operations manager rolled into one.

These positions will not sit within the organization's IT infrastructure, but rather that of its marketing group. They will ultimately report to a chief marketing technologist (CMT)— someone who understands both design and copy but also code and data. These marketing technology teams will manage store environments where marketing and sales are completely integrated and synonymous with the technological customer experience. In companies like this, the greatest IT investments will be made not by the CIO but rather by the CMT..

We're already seeing the crude beginnings of these sorts of environments cropping up in public spaces. Advanced vending machines and automated convenience stores allow for not only immediate dispensing of a growing number of products like electronics, perfume and cosmetics and DVDs, but also for custom orders and delivery. Furthermore, they can handle the end-of-day accounting procedures that are handled manually today.

As these sorts of store environments multiply and increase their footprints, the demand and market value for qualified retail technologists will steadily increase.

The Brand Ambassador

Fully animated experiences, on the other hand, will require the extraordinary work of dynamic individuals who are able to bring the brand's proposition to life. These "brand ambassadors" will, in effect, be the living, breathing embodiment of the brand's beliefs and customs—everything that makes the brand remarkable. They will be engaging individuals who are capable of building strong emotional connections with consumers, and they will be supported by technologies that will help them to achieve this.

Unlike their twentieth-century retail sales ancestors, who were hired largely on the grounds of dependability, friendliness and flexibility, there are three new key competencies required in order to meet the high demands that brand ambassadorship carries with it: believers, super-users and co-creators. The most successful will possess all three.

BELIEVERS, SUPER-USERS AND CO-CREATORS

BELIEVERS   First and foremost, ambassadors must be aligned spiritually and philosophically with the core beliefs of the brand. For the right candidate, his or her association with the brand brings a deep sense of fulfillment, belonging and self-actualization. Every new ambassador brought on board will therefore have a multiplier effect on the level of passion and conviction felt within the brand as a whole.

Brands with a truly galvanized sense of purpose and belief very often don't have to look far for candidates. Candidates themselves will seek out the brands whose interests and values are aligned with their own. Every brand ambassador, therefore, must begin as a believer.

SUPER-USERS   Beyond their alignment with the brand's beliefs and values, ambassadors also need to be super-users of the brand's products and services. They must be intimately familiar with every nuance of what the brand offers, and their expertise must supersede any reasonable amount of information that consumers could gather on their own. Moreover, they have to have the skill to cut through the data, jargon and superfluous stuff and get the customer quickly to where he or she needs to be. The super-users become brand hackers who can guide even the most informed customer.

This doesn't mean super-users will not require additional training; it simply means that from the outset they are wildly passionate and completely familiar with what you sell.

CO-CREATORS   In 1998, Joseph Pine and James Gilmore coauthored the seminal work *The Experience Economy*. The central thesis of the book is that our economy has evolved beyond the process of merely exchanging value for goods and services, and that, increasingly, consumers will pay for experiences. If retailers are to prosper, according to Pine and Gilmore, they will have to become adept at staging in-store experiences that will offer compelling value beyond the physical goods or services.

Since *The Experience Economy* was published, there has been ample evidence of this sort of "retail theater" manifesting itself in the market. From The Disney Store to Whole Foods, retailers have carved out a distinct place in the consumer's mind by animating their stores to go beyond simple distribution.

The next evolution of experiential retailing, however, is to bring consumers from the audience to the stage, personally involving them in the experience as coproducers of their own customized products or services.

The concept of co-creation, once largely associated with online retail, will become a fundamental aspect of the fully animated retail store environment. Brand ambassadors, armed with the tools and technology they need, will have to work intimately with customers to build product and service options that are best suited to the customer's unique needs, and these expert salespeople will do it with the customer's involvement.

———

Some might look at the hiring imperatives of belief, super-use and co-creation as having almost cultish undertones. Frankly that may not be completely unfounded. A cult, despite the negative connotations, is really nothing more than a group of people who are tightly bound together by a particular ideal or belief. Moreover, regardless of how we might characterize these new levels of brand/employee devotion, the employees of the highest-performing companies in the world (Apple, Starbucks, Whole Foods and others) exhibit each of the three key competencies.

So, if we agree that the retail employee of the future possesses this very different skill set, we must next establish how to go about recruiting, cultivating and rewarding this new and elevated class of retail performer. Fortunately there are brands we can look to that are doing just that.

Believers

WESTJET   When you arrive outside the offices of Canadian airline WestJet, don't be shocked to find yourself in the middle of a colossal game of road hockey. "We have a WestJet road hockey league with more than a dozen teams. Our people really love it," says Richard Bartrem, WestJet's vice-president of communications and community relations, as he leads me through the company's bright, airy offices located outside Calgary, Alberta. What you very quickly realize about WestJet, however, is that road hockey isn't the only thing WestJet employees are passionate about.

In an industry characterized by low profitability, labor strife and even bankruptcy, WestJet has managed to achieve extraordinarily consistent and profitable growth since entering the Canadian market in 1996. Despite turbulent economics, tough competition and challenges along the way, the brand now controls a 36-percent share of the market, and doesn't appear to be stopping for breath.

Perhaps the most striking thing about WestJet is the unity of response you get, regardless of whom you speak with, when you ask about what has made the company so successful. The answer is always "our people" — or WestJetters, as they prefer to be called. And while there's no shortage of brands out there that claim to value their people, at WestJet the value is tangible, public and reinforced at every turn.

Bob Cummings, WestJet's executive vice-president, fluently recites the brand's guiding principles off the top of his head. As he does, one can't help but notice that they all in some way relate back to the value of WestJetters.

He explains that central to everything is the brand's belief that friendly, personalized service is what sets the company apart from competition and leaves a lasting emotional connection with their "guests." The first key principle, therefore, is to seek out people who share this belief and ensure that their interests and those of the company are aligned. As part of this system of shared beliefs, the company offers its people unique compensation opportunities, outstanding personal recognition and an enormous degree of ownership in brand decisions.

First, the company offers a lucrative profit-sharing and stock-purchase plan, giving WestJetters a direct interest in the company's growth and profitability. This elevation from employee to shareholder is intrinsic to the employees' rela tionship with the brand and their sense of holding a vested stake in its future.

Second, WestJet has made a habit of sharing ideas with frontline WestJetters first before proceeding with any major strategic decision. These decisions are often significant, such as the recent plan to launch a regional airline, which is now set to go ahead in 2013. Bartrem and Cummings say quite flatly that had employees been against the idea, it simply would not have gone ahead. As a matter fact, they say, *no* new product or service is introduced to market without upfront design and execution input from employees to ensure that it meets their requirements and high standards.

To celebrate this alignment of beliefs, the company holds a staggering 250 employee events each year—150 of which include families! Specific events are held to celebrate what WestJet calls "kudos"—stories of remarkable customer service and compassion received directly from their guests.

WestJetters are also given enormous latitude to use their judgment to make their guests happy, and both Bartrem and Cummings are quick to relate stories of amazing kindness and above-the-call service provided by WestJetters across the country.

"The plane," says Bartrem "is really just the metal tube that gets you from one place to another. It's the friendliness of the people who get you there that our guests remember most."

This fervent core belief in personal, friendly service is what has come to define the WestJet brand and galvanize its culture.

There's no app for empathy.

ZAPPOS.COM Few could have envisioned that a Las Vegas–based online shoe retailer with revenues of a little more than a million and a half dollars in 1999 would become the behemoth that it is today. Zappos's growth has become a thing of legend. But when asked to put a finger on the core cause, CEO Tony Hsieh won't talk about page views, conversion rates or algorithms. Instead and without hesitation, he points to the unique Zappos culture, which is founded on the following 10 core values:

1. Deliver WOW through service
2. Embrace and drive change
3. Create fun and a little weirdness
4. Be adventurous, creative and open-minded
5. Pursue growth and learning
6. Build open and honest relationships with communication
7. Build a positive team and family spirit
8. Do more with less
9. Be passionate and determined
10. Be humble

But unlike other CEOs, many of whom claim to have strongly held values, Hsieh is willing to lose money because of them—$2,000 at a time. The company offers what it calls a "quit bonus" to any new employee who opts to leave the company before completing their training. For Hsieh and the team at Zappos, it's a direct means of weeding out those people who don't truly fit the company's values and beliefs. It's an inexpensive way to keep the culture intact. For those who turn down the quit bonus, it becomes a very public declaration of their alignment with the brand and belief in the core values. Incidentally, over 97 percent of those who are offered the quit bonus refuse it.

Employees continue to publicly declare their belief in the core values on an annual basis. Each year the company publishes what it calls a culture book, which includes completely unedited comments from employees that describe the brand in their own words.

It's also important to appreciate that 75 percent of what Zappos sells is transacted without any intervention from a human customer service representative. It's purely consumer initiated and transacted online. So, why the emphasis on people? All the more reason, says Hsieh, to be sure that the people manning the other 25 percent of sales are the best people available. These moments of truth are, in Hsieh's estimation, what truly define the brand.

Scan this to see Tony Hsieh give a short presentation on how Zappos creates a great organizational culture.

But does all this pay off? You bet it does. Zappos is now part of Amazon.com, and its sales top $1.5 billion, 75 percent of which is delivered by repeat customers. The company has a voluntary employee turnover rate of between 8 percent and 15 percent, depending on the facility—a fraction of what is common in the call center and warehousing industries.

Like WestJet, Zappos has made culture and unity of belief a sustainable and organic competitive advantage.

Super-Users

SEPHORA   You don't have to be a makeup expert to work at one of Sephora's 1,300 cosmetics stores worldwide. You do, however, need to be fanatically in love with makeup! Apart from its bright, busy and visually exciting stores, the secret to Sephora's success lies in its ability to seek out and develop brand super-users into skilled salespeople.

In what is reputed to be up to three weeks of recruitment rigor for store staff, Sephora puts candidates through their paces in an effort to establish just how deep their love for beauty products and their ability to share that love really runs. Multiple interviews and additional testing are common as the company sifts through to find those with extraordinary passion for Sephora products.

While hourly wages at Sephora tend not to exceed industry averages, staff, eager to get what the company calls "gratis" (Sephora lingo for free stuff) are more than willing to attend company training sessions. The more sessions staff attend, the more gratis they get. The more gratis they get, the more hardcore a super-user they become.

The company also offers "The Science of Sephora," an intensive program aimed at refining employees' knowledge of the company's products and enabling them to perform demonstrations and work with clients.

REI   According to customer experience design expert Mike Wittenstein, outdoor equipment retailer REI is one of the best at leveraging super-users to build "in-store education into its retail experiences in a way that adds value—and adds directly to sales." At REI, Wittenstein says, "sales associates don't 'teach,' they inspire." He adds that part of the power is the visceral nature of the in-store experience. "When it's appropriate, you'll be handling the gear, pitching the tent, holding the paddle, trying on the waders, and so on. Part of good preparation is knowing how your new gear works, feels, and performs." This intense level of advice from a product super-user "helps customers focus their desires, prioritize their purchases, and better clarify their upcoming trip or expedition—all of which makes them more confident shoppers." And that, he says, drives above-average sales, profits and customer satisfaction.[7]

REI CEO Sally Jewell in front of the 65-foot climbing wall at the company's Seattle flagship store. (AP Photo/Scott Cohen)

It's likely no coincidence that REI has appeared on *Fortune* magazine's list of the top 100 companies to work for since the list began in 1998. To some companies this level of fanatical product adoration might seem over the top. But I would argue that in a world where information is free and accessible to the average consumer, only such a level of fanatical super-use can keep your staff more informed than the customer in front of them.

Super-users are not only your best customers—they're your best employees.

Co-creators

FUJITSU   While lines of customers wait outside Apple stores for their pre-built and neatly prepackaged iPhone and iPads, Fujitsu of Japan has taken a very different approach to its technology sales. The company is now offering workshops at its production facilities that enable customers to not only customize but also assemble their computers themselves! The workshops, led by expert Fujitsu engineers, offer customers the opportunity to learn about their computers as they construct them. They can even engrave their own name into its case. All computers are thoroughly inspected by Fujitsu engineering staff for quality before leaving the facility.

While the idea of assembling one's own computer might leave some cold, you can bet there's a segment of the market for which this experience would be euphoric. In fact, the company is already planning to expand these workshops into other markets.

STUDIO VELO   With stores in San Francisco and Mill Valley, California, Studio Velo is, by many accounts, the ultimate cyclist's paradise. Online reviews of the shop include testimonials like: "The best bike shop I've ever been to"; "LOVE, LOVE, LOVE Studio Velo"; and, my personal favorite, "The whole shop kicks ass!"

Apart from a focus on great products, what Studio Velo discovered early is that its customers aren't just buying a bike—they're paying to be part of a unique experience. And Studio Velo has created the perfect experience for its customers.

Using a state-of-the-art 3-D motion capture system and what the chain hails as the first "robotic assisted fitting system," customers are able to mod, tweak and tune their new bike to exactly the right specifications. Consumers therefore aren't just buying a bike, they're helping to *create* their bike.

Both Fujitsu and Studio Velo are tapping a deep need on the part of customers to move beyond being mere consumers and to experience the joy of co-creation. This fun and collaborative level of personalization offers a means of building a deep emotional connection with their brands.

A TRULY HUMAN RESOURCE

So the future of retailing brings with it a few completely new imperatives for the retail organization:

- First, it must choose clearly between staging fully automated retail experiences and fully animated ones.
- Second, it must ensure that whichever experience it chooses, it is truly remarkable.
- Third, it must fuel these experiences with bright, talented retail technologists or brand ambassadors—a completely new breed of frontline retail employee.

This, of course, sets off a series of implications for human resources professionals in the retail industry. A total recalibration of their recruitment and compensation models is required in preparation for what will be an entirely different retail market.

Today, the goal in most chains is to find *store associates* (preferably with a pulse) who demonstrate reasonable dependability, trustworthiness and intellect. Most chains use minimum wage as the baseline from which to build store compensation plans. Most companies anticipate and accept high turnover rates and training costs as a part of doing business. And most are settling for just average and even below-average performance.

In the new era, however, the objective will be to attract, nurture and reward retail technologists and brand ambassadors who have vastly different and significantly more evolved skills. Unlike the store associate of today, these new retail champions will possess outstanding talent, unique characters and high personal standards for performance. They will be people who love what you sell and, more importantly, love *why* you sell it. They will be protective of your brand (often more protective than you) and equally protective of their ability to perform their work with autonomy and trust. They will be generous co-creators eager to share their passion with others. They will be living breathing evangelists for your brand, creating moments of magic both through advanced technology and their own unique spirit. And make no mistake, they will command significant market value for their extraordinary talents—a value that has no relationship to minimum wage. Your entire attitude toward compensation and turnover will change dramatically when your prized employees are receiving employment offers from rival retailers.

Far from dehumanizing, the rehumanization of retail is fast approaching. For brands, employees and consumers alike, it's the beginning of a new and astonishing era in retailing—the true golden age. But, it means first accepting that the days of the unskilled and underpaid store clerk are over.

8

The Third Shelf

THE RETAIL UNIVERSE has always operated on the premise of there being "two shelves." The first shelf is the store shelf, where customers happily peruse goods and compare prices, quality and color until they come to a decision to buy something. The elated consumer then goes home or to his or her workplace and deposits the product on the second shelf, where it is used or consumed. Two shelves.

For centuries, marketers have been attempting to better understand the consumer's thought processes and behaviors when in front of these two shelves. They've invested untold time, money and energy to uncover the triggers that motivate purchase behavior off the retailer's shelf, and repeat purchase behavior from the consumer's shelf. It hasn't mattered whether the product is life insurance, jelly beans or automobiles, for marketers everywhere, a significant percentage of their work and attention has revolved and continues to revolve around these two shelves.

In between these two physical shelves exists the nebulous continuum of time and space that we've come to call the consumer's *path to purchase*—or, the intellectual, emotional and physical journey that consumers make to buy the things they want and need. We marketers have tried to break the path down into recognizable and measurable stages: initial realization of need, exploration of brand and product alternatives, development of brand awareness, generation of brand interest, motivation to buy, purchase and (hopefully) repeat purchase and advocacy. The stages of the path can vary depending on whom you ask, but just about every marketer will agree that it can be a long and complex journey, rife with competitors all vying for the precious attention of meandering consumers.

Without many better alternatives, marketers have historically resorted to carpet bombing this path with advertising— mostly mass in nature—in an attempt to arrest consumer attention just long enough to extol the virtues of their products before their competitors could do the same, and with the same ubiquitous slogans: "We're number one in customer satisfaction—for three years in a row!" "Our product is rated number one by J. D. Power and Associates—there's no reason to buy from anyone else!" "Buy from the best. Forget the rest!" Whoever could lead the largest assault with this sort of advertising usually won the war for consumers.

Of course, as media channels and demographics became more fragmented, new and more sophisticated artillery was required to identify and target elusive consumers within the broader market. Psychographic clustering enabled a somewhat better, thinner slicing of segments, and specialty media formats like cable TV and niche magazines allowed for a slightly more surgical approach. But despite evolving tactics, the core message remained the same, "We're the best; come and buy from us!" The marketing objective, too, was unwavering: get the consumer to notice you (your brand), woo the consumer with words and hurry the consumer down the path to purchase into your brand's waiting arms.

Then, one day, advertising became a dirty word, and was replaced by the less-descript but far more fashionable term *engagement*. Brands no longer advertised *to* consumers, they engaged *with* them. The crude message "We're the best; come and buy from us!" was replaced with more creative evocations like, "Listen to our amazing story and love us!"; "Watch our funny video and talk to us!"; or "Play our fun game and tell someone about us!" Marketing shifted from pitchy push to creative pull. The idea being that the engaged consumer will become a buying consumer…eventually…right?

This is all well and good, and for a while it was somewhat novel, except that now instead of a barrage of advertising, consumers face an ever-escalating litany of marketing aimed at *engaging* them! We're literally OD'ing on engagement! Try, over an average day, to keep track of how many brands appeal to you to engage with them: *text this number, scan this code, watch this video, share this story, write a review, visit our Facebook page*—the list is endless! It seems that being engaged could easily become a full-time job. Moreover, a recent study by IBM found that while upwards of 60 percent of executives believed that customers followed their brands on social media sites to be part of their brand community (a.k.a. to be engaged) only 25 to 30 percent of customers felt the same way. In fact, most just wanted a discount.[1]

The real underlying problem is that most of this engagement leads us to exactly the same end point that the crappy old advertising did—to a store, a website or a mobile app, all in the hope of heightening our interest with yet more information and crafty content. It makes one wonder if engagement hasn't simply become the *new advertising*.

And then there's the question of effectiveness. A recent global survey from Nielsen of over 28,000 consumers concluded that a full 92 percent trust word-of-mouth recommendations from friends and family above all other forms of brand messaging—an increase of 18 percent since 2007. So until a consumer actually buys your product or service, what is there to talk about? How will your brand garner word-of-mouth recommendations if there are no mouths talking about you?

The irony is that, in the meantime, we've seen the development of a mind-bending array of new and amazing tools, not only to interact but also to transact with consumers in a very different way—to alter the way we intersect with them along the path to purchase. Yet many marketers are simply carrying the same old tactics and strategies over to these new mediums. It's happening constantly. YouTube videos are used merely to redirect consumers to online stores. Facebook pages are simply herding consumers toward physical store locations, and mobile apps are wasted in supplying a sea of coupons to be used at some downstream distribution point. Is this really the best we can do? I don't think so, and that's why I'm suggesting that you begin thinking now about an entirely different approach.

While most businesses remain mired in the parochial question of where to *advertise* (oops, sorry...*engage*) and how better to assail customers through various media channels, I encourage you and anyone else who will listen to do what enlightened businesses have already begun doing: building something I call the *third shelf*.

THE ARRIVAL OF THE THIRD SHELF

In June 2011, a video began making its way through the retail and marketing circles on Twitter. It was produced by British multinational grocery giant Tesco, and it documented a project the chain had launched in South Korea, where Tesco's Homeplus chain of stores occupies the number two market position behind competitor E-Mart.

The challenge facing Tesco was figuring out how to grow market share without adding more stores in an already dense marketplace.

Commuters stroll past one of Homeplus' virtual stores.
(Paul Brown / Rex Features)

In exploring possibilities, Tesco arrived at two important cultural insights into the Korean market: First, that about one in two South Koreans are smartphone users—an astonishing percentage.[2] And second, that the citizens of Seoul spent an inordinate amount of time working and commuting. Over 4 million people were riding the subway in the city of Seoul each day, and the commute left little free time to shop for groceries and other needs.[3] The unarticulated consumer pain point, therefore, was not a lack of stores in the marketplace, but rather a terrible lack of time to shop.

With that in mind, Tesco took an entirely different approach to growing its market share. It installed immense graphics on the subway walls that perfectly replicated the look of nicely merchandised grocery store shelves. Hundreds of products, including meat, dairy, fresh produce and packaged goods, were all graphically represented with high-definition photography. Below each product was a quick response (QR) code that tied to that specific product. The video showed waiting commuters walking the length of these huge signs, scanning items as they went and adding them to an online shopping cart. Shoppers could then pay for their order and schedule a time for home delivery later that day.

As the video circulated, much of the discussion from the marketing community centered on what most saw as a creative and novel use of technology on Tesco's part. For others, myself included, it represented something far more profound, fundamental and historic. It was as though the tectonic plates of the retail industry were shifting under foot. What Tesco had so brilliantly done was create a completely new and legitimate buying channel. It had discovered the *third shelf*—a place that was not the store and not the customer's home, but a third and wonderfully appropriate location for its consumers to shop. And what's more, this wasn't merely a pop-up novelty promotion. This was a full-blown store without the wages, inventory, utility bills or real estate taxes! And if that wasn't good enough, the damn thing actually worked! Over 10,000 shoppers bought from the online Homeplus store using smartphones. The number of Homeplus registered shoppers rose by 76 percent, and online sales increased by 130 percent.

Given the success of the Korean commuter test, Tesco has moved ahead with another similar installation, this time in the UK's Gatwick Airport. The setup allows passengers to order from 80 common food items—the kinds of things you might not feel like picking up at the store after a long trip. Once paid for, the items can be scheduled for delivery. And others are following Tesco's lead, building similar sorts of virtual shopping installations around the world.

What Tesco and a growing number of others have discovered is technology's unprecedented ability to create functional digital stores that can be strategically positioned along the consumer's path to purchase. They aren't merely engaging them or advertising to them, they are enabling them to buy to fill their needs—to *transact*! At the same time, as they've discovered, these third shelves spin off significant word-of-mouth advertising and media attention.

So, while some retail industry observers regarded the Tesco experiment in isolation and as a novelty, the rest of us saw it as a watershed moment in which the very concept of *what a store is* and how consumers engage with it had been redefined.

You see, the elephant in the room is that deep down, not only do consumers *not* want to be advertised to, our time and tolerance for engagement is also limited. How many of us really want engagement from the brand or retailer that sells us soap, toothpaste, shoes or any number of other everyday items? How many of us have liked a brand's Facebook page, only to *unlike* it months later when the engagement simply became obnoxious, too frequent or tiresome?

In truth, what we *do* want are the products and services we need, at the exact instant we need them, wherever we happen to be. And here's the thing: for the first time in the history of retailing, brands have the power to deliver exactly that!

THE STORE IS EVERYWHERE

Today, the competitive geography in retail is pretty easy to navigate. There are physical stores, web stores and mobile applications that sometimes tie the two together. But technology is blurring the lines between these retail spaces, and it's not hard to imagine a future retail landscape that looks unlike anything we see around us today.

For example, imagine driving a huge moving van outfitted with retail fixtures, signs, a cash register and loads of jewelry up Fifth Avenue in Manhattan, and parking directly in front of Tiffany & Co. You could swing open the doors and sell to the throngs of people passing by — 24 hours a day, seven days a week. You could make a fortune and never pay a penny in wages or rent. Best of all, there's nothing Tiffany can do to stop you.

Sounds preposterous right? And in the physical world it would be, but in the world of augmented reality (A/R), it's entirely possible, and, to a growing extent, it's happening already.

An augmented (or virtual) reality experience is nothing more than digital content that is overlaying a physical object or location where consumers can then interact with it. It occupies no physical space, but it is every bit as *real* and interactive as a physical store.

Augmented reality applications like Layar, Blippar and others are already giving brands the capability to launch virtual experiences wherever they want, provided there's enough signal for mobile users to interact with them. Businesses like Disney and Nike have already experimented with the technology. With some basic web-programming skills, almost anyone can create digital content and place it just about anywhere in the physical realm, including at some of the most prestigious shopping avenues in the world. In fact, French clothing brand Hostage Wear has opened over 20 A/R shops in some of the world's best-known venues, including Piccadilly Circus, Red Square, Venice Beach and Madison Square Park. Slowly but very surely the world is being populated with stores that only smart mobile devices can see.

 Scan this to watch a short clip where I explain the third shelf concept.

This raises some thought-provoking questions about the eventual meeting point between digital content and physical location. As augmented reality increases in usage, could we see potential turf wars between physical and digital retail experiences, with businesses vying for consumer attention in the same locations? Case in point: Chinese grocery chain Yihaodian recently revealed plans to create up to 1,000 virtual augmented reality stores, including some directly at their competitors' physical locations! So, it's not hard to imagine a world where Mercedes-Benz establishes virtual showrooms outside BMW physical showrooms, or vice versa. Where Coke creates virtual stores using the Pepsi logo as the image-recognition trigger for the experience. Where Macy's uses the sound of a Sears commercial as the audible catalyst for a virtual store experience. You get the picture. There are currently no limitations on any of this. Your store can now be wherever you want it to be—up to and including inside a competitor's store!

With every passing week, we are seeing new third shelf opportunities arise that further challenge our concept of what a store is and can be. Smart brands are pushing the envelope of how and where they can intersect with purchase-ready consumers. Here are just a few.

- **"Shopable" Video:** Hip-hop artists FKi, Iggy Azalea and Diplo recently released an online video for the song "I Think She Ready." The video actually enables viewers to purchase different items of clothing that the artists wear in the production, while watching the video itself. Simply by hovering their mouse over a fashion look they like, viewers can be instantly transported to an interface for online retailer Ssense.com, which allows them to buy the item and then return quite seamlessly to watching the video.

- **Virtual Stores:** When Net-A-Porter launched the new Karl Lagerfeld clothing collection, it did so by wrapping the windows of select physical store locations in major cities around the world with images of the collection. The only thing was, the stores held no product, employed no staff and never even opened their doors. Instead, passersby could purchase items from the store instantly, 24 hours a day, simply by viewing the images on the storefront with their mobile devices and placing an order for delivery. The line sold out in two days.

- **Second Screen Experiences:** eBay recently piloted an app called Watch With eBay, which, when synced with a local television provider's programming schedule, allows users to instantly find merchandise on eBay that is directly related to the show they happen to be watching. The Giants fan watching the game could now shop for fan gear in the heat of the moment! *Twilight* fanatics could buy Edward Cullen T-shirts while watching the movie— for the fourth time.

- **Direct Sales:** Evian water created a device that allows its Parisian consumers, with the touch of a button, to order more mineral water directly from Evian. The device simply attaches magnetically to their fridge and, when pushed, places a direct order with Evian for delivery to the consumer's home.

- **Mobile Stores:** Procter & Gamble has launched a concept in New York City that allows consumers to shop for some of the organization's most popular items by scanning large QR codes on the sides of trucks that tour around to various high-foot-traffic locales in the city. Fulfillment is handled by Walmart, with free delivery to the customer's home on orders exceeding $45.

- **Social Shops:** Facebook is getting ready to release its Facebook Gifts program, which notifies Facebook users of friends' birthdays and provides them with the option of sending the friend a real-world gift! Facebook is in the process of gathering partners for this program as I write this.

- **Post-purchase:** Augmented reality platforms are enabling brands like Cadbury, Heinz and others to turn their own product packaging into an interactive experience. For example, if you notice that you're running out of ketchup, you could conceivably use the label on your nearly empty bottle to access the product's virtual store to order more. In other words, the product itself has the potential to become the store!

As you can see, creating third shelf opportunities isn't as easy or straightforward as simply moving money out of conventional channels and into digital, mobile or online ones. In fact, it may involve mashing them all together. The third shelf can be a physical or a virtual place. It can be mobile or it can be a fixed location brought to life by mobile devices. It can be digital media, or print media infused with digital functionality. In truth, it can be just about anything you, the brand, want.

But it starts by asking new questions that have nothing to do with mediums, channels or devices. The question every marketer needs to answer is this: *When and where in the world are consumers when they are considering or in need of the things we sell?* And that question applies regardless of what you sell. Where and when do people think about buying a new car? When do people feel the unshakable need to take a vacation, and where are they precisely when that feeling hits them? What are the events in a person's life leading up to buying a child's education fund or a life insurance policy? Simply, where are consumers when they need you, and how can you transport your offering to them at that exact moment?

Once you determine the answer to that most primary of questions, then and only then should you begin to consider the combination of mediums, channels and devices—and even physical surfaces within the environment (like subway walls)—that can be utilized to create an effective third shelf.

For retailers there's some important writing on the wall here: brands now have the power to take their own products to the physical local market without relying on brick-and-mortar stores for distribution. So you'd be wise to begin constructing your third shelf, before your vendors construct theirs.

In the new age of consumerism, the world is now your store.

WHERE'S YOUR THIRD SHELF?

I can say with relative certainty that regardless of what you sell, there's an opportunity for you to create a logical and compelling third shelf where consumers can buy from you. The only question is *where*.

The knee-jerk response, of course, is likely to be places where there are lots and lots of people. It's natural to default to busy places like bus and train stations, airports, hotels, etc. As marketers and retailers, we've gotten into the habit of gravitating to the greatest number of eyeballs for our messages. We've been raised in a world of impressions, page views and foot traffic.

Unfortunately, this approach to market requires an entirely new methodology. It's not about number of impressions, but rather about the volume of shared need—the likelihood that consumers in a given place, at a given time, will need what you sell and being willing and able to buy it. The goal is not to interrupt customers with something they don't care about, it's to be available to provide something they consciously or unconsciously need already.

For example, you manage a drug store and notice that air travelers are arriving last-minute to buy toiletries. The opportunity to meet this need for those who don't have the time to get to a store is to erect a virtual store at airport gates, allowing people to quickly and easily order a pre-packed toiletries kit in the departing airport for pickup at the arrival gate in the destination airport. Smooth, seamless and tangibly valuable.

According to Gary Schwartz, author of *The Impulse Economy* and *Fast Shopper, Slow Store*, "The whole concept of *path to purchase* has changed with the connected consumer. It has always been a perilous path, but with an always-on mobile shopper, purchase (in many cases) can happen without the path. For this digital generation, they are already fully researched online and ready to make a purchase decision. Google calls this the ZERO MOMENT OF TRUTH (Z-MOT)—If the shopper is in the market for a dishwasher, they have already scoured the web for information on the best product at the best price."[4]

If the store or brand can make a purchase of a dishwasher simple at a bus shelter or billboard, then the shopper is highly likely to act on this advertisement. The path to purchase becomes an actual purchase.

So, somewhere along your customer's path to purchase, there are points where they will likely cut to the chase and buy from you. Once you believe you've uncovered times and spaces that fit your third shelf criteria, you need to evaluate them against three important success factors. They are *relevance*, *familiarity* and *context*.

Relevance

Tesco's third shelf experiment in Korea worked because it offered a shopping experience that was highly satisfactory for commuters—the ease of grocery shopping while waiting for the next train was time saving and convenient. The first key for marketers, therefore, lies in deconstructing the path to purchase to find moments in consumers' lives where they are predisposed to buying what you sell. In Tesco's case, one of these moments happened to be while consumers were commuting to and from work, and this just happened to take the installation into the subway. The point is that Tesco used a significant revelation about the Korean consumer's path to purchase, and worked that back to find the right location for their third shelf, not the other way around.

Now compare this to a similar installation from German shoe retailer Goertz Shoes. Using the Microsoft Kinect technology, Goertz enabled passing shoppers to try on any pair of shoes in its collection in a virtual way, viewable in 3-D on a large screen. If the user found a pair of shoes he or she liked, the purchase could be made by scanning a QR code that linked the shopper to an online store. Also, like Tesco, the chain chose a busy train station (in this case in Hamburg) for its test.

But unlike Tesco, the Goertz experiment didn't garner much reaction or attention. No one was overly excited about it. The reason, it seems to me, is that while it was a really cool idea and well implemented, it lacked any true relevance to consumers in that particular situation. It's hard to know what insights guided the project, but I've never seen anything that would lead me to believe that a high percentage of consumers are preoccupied with shopping for new footwear while they're in train stations.

On the other hand, I recently met a woman at a conference I was speaking at who was trying desperately to get distribution for a new and innovative form of mosquito repellant. She'd been trying to no avail to get listed with major retailers. Moreover, she was quickly running out of options to get what she saw as a breakthrough product into the hands of consumers before running out of capital to fund the venture. I suggested that rather than submitting to more rejection at retail, she consider taking her product directly to consumers when they're firstly, most likely to be open and receptive to information on a great mosquito repellant and secondly, willing to pay just about any price to get it. That place was wherever consumers were being eaten alive by mosquitos. So rather than beating her head against retailers' doors, I suggested she work to get an agreement with some of North America's major campground operators to build virtual stores, where campers could order her product online and have it delivered directly to their campsite. Why depend on conventional means of distribution when you have the ability to take the store directly to the customer? If consumers wanted her product badly enough, they'd absorb the shipping costs and if her product was really as good as she said it was, consumers would eventually be going to established stores and asking for it.

If you can isolate the moment(s) in a consumer's life when they *really* need your product, for the first time in history, you have the technological ability to be there at that exact instant and make the sale.

Familiarity

The second critical aspect of the Tesco experiment in Korea was ensuring that elements of the user interface felt familiar to shoppers. The grocery shelves were deliberately identical in every respect to what they'd see in store. Products were life-size. Tesco even merchandised duplicate products side by side, if that was what shoppers would normally expect to see in their local store. Next, Tesco laid everything out so that shoppers could walk down the length of the virtual aisle just as they would shop in a real-world store. By building familiar shopping behaviors into the interface, Tesco eliminated much of the confusion and cool response that can result from asking consumers to adopt new or unfamiliar practices or behaviors in order to participate.

In a similar sense, German pet food manufacturer GranataPet created an installation that brought billboards, geolocation technology, social media and good old-fashioned product sampling together. The brand installed billboards along a heavily traveled dog-walking route. The billboard carried the message, "Check in to snack out," and invited Foursquare users who happened to be walking their dogs to check in at the location of the billboard. Each time an owner did so, the billboard released a small sample of GranataPet dog food into a bowl below it, for the dog to dig into—which of course most dogs were more than happy to do!

In this case, not only did the brand get its product into the customer's hands (or dog's mouth, as it were), it also capitalized on the social buzz that was created around the check-ins and subsequent online chatter they created. Again, GranataPet was wise to build a familiar behavior into an unfamiliar concept. By using something as simple as a Foursquare check-in, they reduced behavioral friction significantly.

Building known and familiar behaviors into your third shelf, regardless of where it is, will help it gain significantly greater trial and adoption.

Context

The last thing that the Tesco experience teaches retailers and marketers is the importance of ensuring the experience is contextually convenient and permissible for consumers to engage in. There would be little point in giving consumers an opportunity to shop your product in a situation that doesn't afford them the time to do so. It's critical that they have the time, desire and capability to shop to such an extent that it creates definable value.

To illustrate the difference, take the examples of the Ford Fiesta and the Chevy Volt. Ford recently launched what it called a Go-Further pop-up shop in San Francisco's Union Square. The shop was a display of art, fashion, food and design, all aimed at telling a story about some of the new approaches that Ford is taking in the design and construction of its vehicles. The centerpiece of the exhibit was a sneak peak at the 2013 Ford Fiesta. The brand's stated objectives were increased awareness and consideration of their products.

There's little doubt that the exhibit would have attracted some attention and certainly even resulted in some positive impressions. That said, installations like this are still somewhat reflective of the old-school approach of commandeering consumer attention, pushing a message with arguable relevance and packaging it up in an experience that is largely non-contextual and interruptive in nature. One has to wonder what percentage of people aimlessly passing through Union Square would be willing to receive information about a new model of Ford automobile. My guess is not many. For a number of people, the promotion would feel like nothing more than a bit of a sideshow and an interruption to their day.

Compare this to the concept that a Brazilian car dealer, Orca Chevrolet, came up with to introduce the new Chevy Volt in its market. Orca partnered with a local towing company to offer rides and even test-drives in a brand-new Chevy Volt to stranded motorists whose cars had broken down at the side of the road. Chevy Volts would literally follow these tow trucks from breakdown to breakdown. Can you think of a more contextually appropriate time to introduce a new car model than when people are following behind their junker as it's being towed away? The audience size, of course, would have been fractional compared to the Ford event, but the level of context is incomparably higher.[5]

So, it's absolutely critical to ensure that your third shelf concept is contextually aligned with the time and place in a practical sense, which results in an openness and willingness of consumers to consider and buy.

And what can retail brands do to stake out their digital space? Maarten Lens-FitzGerald, co-founder of Layar, recommends "not approaching the issue from a defensive position." He maintains that brands should be developing augmented reality experiences *now*, even if they don't have the longer-term strategy in place. They should at least begin developing an approach. He points out that with the advent of mobile applications that organize nearby virtual content according to popularity and relevance, low-quality content and experiences will simply fall to the bottom of the list. In the end, he maintains, whoever "owns the best experience" will win.[6]

BUYING EATS ENGAGING FOR BREAKFAST

So while most companies are still obsessing about where to advertise and how to engage consumers, smart companies are microscopically exploring their consumer's path to find the key life moments and places where the combination of relevant products, familiar interfaces and contextually appropriate environments add up to a high degree of interest, need and willingness to buy. They are creatively pulling together combinations of media, channels and devices to facilitate these new and game-changing store concepts.

The big idea in all of this is that, for the first time ever, retailers and brands have the ability to go beyond merely advertising to or even engaging with consumers. Technology has given them the capacity to set up shop at any point they want along the path to purchase. They no longer have to pin all their hopes on reaching the consumer at the two conventional shelves, or fruitlessly barrage consumers on the path to purchase. They can turn every piece of marketing into an opportunity to actually SELL THINGS, when and where consumers need them, using these and other creative third shelf innovations.

Frankly, if I'm looking for a way for customers to understand my brand story, love my products and service and build a sense of loyalty, I'll choose them buying from me over engaging with me any day. If we're honest about it, buying (not likes, follows or page views) is the highest form of engagement a consumer can have with a brand.

Stop Thinking Channels and Devices
Start Thinking Moments and Surfaces

This unprecedented capability to transport buying opportunities to consumers wherever they may be begs a wholesale rethinking of how we go to market.

Historically marketers have obsessed over which channels, mediums and devices to use to push their messages through to consumers. Little regard was given beyond driving the marketing message down the pipe to reach the consumer, garner an impression and hopefully spark some action further down the path to purchase.

Today's marketer should instead be thinking more in terms of identifying the precise moments, instances, occasions and snippets of time in a consumer's life when they genuinely need what's being sold. This could be anywhere and I'm willing to bet it's not where you're currently spending most of your marketing budget. This means, rather than simply looking for the biggest target audience, marketers need to do the detailed work of dissecting the consumer's life to discover these super-relevant moments where they are most in need of what you sell. Once identified, the objective becomes not to market but to sell to consumers exactly then! Not to get them to listen or engage but to buy.

Marketers would also be wise to stop thinking in terms of device strategies—mobile, tablet, etc. and think instead in terms of *surfaces*. What surfaces are available and contextual in these identified moments when your consumer needs you?

What mix of surfaces and technologies can be used in conjunction with one another to form a familiar feeling shopping opportunity. For example, if most of your customers happen to be waiting to board planes when they realize they need you, what combination of surfaces and technology at an airport gate could be used to build a contextually appropriate buying opportunity? The ideal solution will most likely be a mix of available surfaces and devices. But don't limit your thinking to conventional channels and single device strategies. Those chains have been broken.

The days of retailers haplessly waiting like hitchhikers along the path to purchase are over. Your brand can be transported anywhere customers are waiting to buy. The time has come for all brands to claim their space on the third shelf—wherever that may be.

9

The Destination Is You

RECENTLY, I CAME ACROSS an article about a Washington, DC, hospital that was experiencing a high rate of readmissions among patients treated and released from its emergency department. Intuitively, doctors at the hospital felt that many readmissions could have been prevented with better follow-up care, but no one could identify which patients might be most at risk for readmission and why. The issue became even more urgent on the heels of an announcement by Medicare that hospitals would be penalized for every readmission within 30 days of discharge.

The hospital turned to an unlikely resource in Eric Horvitz, a Microsoft computer scientist and physician. Horvitz and his team built an analytic model that examined data from over 300,000 ER visits and evaluated those visits against 25,000 unique variables including the patient's condition, medical history and attending physician.

Amid the sea of data, Horvitz found hidden correlations. The first had to do with the patient's length of stay in hospital. He found that patients with a stay extending beyond 14 hours were far more likely to be readmitted. The second correlation was related to fluid: any patient whose chart was inscribed with the word "fluid" was more likely to experience a health concern that would require a return trip to the hospital. With these two insights, doctors at Washington Hospital Center could anticipate and minimize instances of readmission.

The work that Horvitz did was later built into a Microsoft program called Readmissions Manager, which analyzes massive amounts of patient data to flag correlations between specific conditions and risk of readmission. This analysis enables medical staff to take preventative action, thus mitigating a problem that costs Medicare $17 billion annually.[1]

So why begin a chapter in a book about retail with an anecdote that appears to have very little to do with the subject? Because, in fact, this story has *everything* to do with retail. The problems faced by Washington Hospital Center were the very same problems that have plagued the retail industry since Henry Walton Smith opened the first chain of bookstores in 1792. That problem is this: retailers are unable to understand the important correlations and cause-and-effect relationships hidden within the mountains of data flowing through their operations every day. Why certain things sell and others don't. Why one staff member outperforms all others. Why specific customers are more profitable than the rest. These and similar questions have been put on the table and solutions guessed at (often incorrectly) for hundreds of years.

───────

WHAT'S THE BIG DEAL ABOUT BIG DATA?

That has changed thanks to something called *big data*—a capability of machinating and manipulating mountains of mind-boggling information in order to find hidden logic and connections between disparate pieces of data. And companies are spending *loads* of money on it.

According to research from Edgell Knowledge Network (EKN), 80 percent of executives who work for major retail companies are aware of big data. The bad news is that about 50 percent of executives don't understand what big data can do for their business. And the scary part is that despite possessing such a nascent understanding, nearly 60 percent of retailers surveyed already have a big data strategy or plan to build one. Yikes! This is like running briskly into the fog, as they say.

Nonetheless, big data has become retail's *really big* story, and will unquestionably be a source of *big* revenue for technology companies. But the question is, what *is* big data and why does it matter so much?

Let's start at what is indisputable: the sheer amount of data being produced in the world today is staggering. Each year more data is generated than was created between the dawn of mankind and 2003. Let's put that into other terms that might be more digestible. Every year, the global store of data doubles. In 2011 alone, the world produced or replicated an astounding 1.8 zettabytes of data. Still not feeling it? Let's put it this way, to store 1.8 zettabytes of data you would need a pile of 32G iPads 25 times higher than Mount Fuji.[2]

For retail companies, this data takes two forms. First, there's structured data (sales, transactions, profit margins, etc.), which most people are perfectly comfortable with and accustomed to capturing and analyzing. Retailers are not as advanced with analysis of unstructured data (social media dialogue, blogs, traffic, weather, store video, competitor activity, etc.). It's worth mentioning that an estimated 80 percent of the data relevant to the operation of companies is, in fact, unstructured data.

So, the belief is that if one could mine and make sense of this treasure trove of unstructured data, retailers could learn a tremendous amount about their operations and ultimately how better to identify, market to and service their target consumers.

But big data is hardly new. Amazon.com has worked with massive amounts of data for years, using it to build personal recommendations for its customers. It's becoming scalable, however, thanks to *in-memory* (a.k.a super-fast) computing and *Hadoop* (a.k.a super robust and flexible) databases. It is now possible and cost effective to analyze mountains of data faster than ever before. Furthermore, we now have the capacity to find correlations between other pieces of structured and unstructured data—secrets that have long been buried deep in the enterprise. Many of these correlations would simply elude human analytical capacity, largely because too much data must be analyzed to find points of convergence. Connections between weather and store traffic, merchandising and profitability, staffing and productivity, politics and product preferences and just about anything you can imagine is now collectable and decipherable—in a heartbeat. In short, retailers can turn noisy chaotic data into a clear and discernable signal that guides decision-making and tactics and roll those tactics out—not days, weeks or months after the fact—but in real time.

So what kinds of data are companies collecting and analyzing?

- Spanish mobile telecom Telefónica will provide aggregate, anonymous data that outlines the physical movements of its mobile subscribers, who are broken down into segments. In other words, if a clothing chain wanted to discover the daily paths through a city taken by teenage girls, Telefónica can gather and supply the data.[3]

- Mobile app developer ShopSavvy collects detailed data on who is scanning what and where, and even gathers details about who they are and what their credit score is! ShopSavvy then feeds this back out to companies in aggregate form.

- Social media aggregators like Radian6 and Sysomos collect, sift and sort vast amounts of social commentary across multiple social networks, detecting chatter and sentiment around specific topics, brands or products.

- Italian mannequin maker Almax has created clothing mannequins equipped with anonymous facial recognition technology to record the age, gender and race of people passing by shop windows to allow merchants to adjust window displays and record the aggregate reaction of consumers and stopping power of their displays.

- Sporting apparel retailer Foot Locker recently began testing systems to capture and analyze video footage of customer traffic through stores. Their goal is to correlate traffic with sales to establish conversion rates for specific products.

All this data has the potential to provide retailers with insights that simply may never have been possible before, and that can therefore help them avoid jumping to premature and erroneous conclusions about customer behavior.

For example, 10 years ago if a company was selling an item that began to experience a high rate of product returns, it may have rushed to the conclusion that the product was defective or problematic and dropped it from the assortment. However, using big-data analysis, other less obvious correlations might be uncovered. It may be discovered that the majority of returns take place when a specific team of employees is working, suggesting performance or training issues. In other words, it allows a company to go beyond gut feeling or superficial analysis and find hidden connections.

And the payoff? Well, by some estimates, retailers who are diving into and becoming adept with big data stand to improve their operating margins by up to 60 percent. Who can argue with that?

However, despite what may seem like a landslide of positives, some experts argue that big data could in fact cause big problems or just be a big waste of time.

A recent study out of Pew Research found a 50/40 percent split between experts who believe that big data will be a largely positive influence on society and those who believe just the opposite. Those in the positive camp see big data as a way for businesses to create better experiences for their customers by becoming better able to "nowcast" the needs of consumers in real time. Others warn of potential misuses, privacy infractions and the false sense of omniscience that big data can cause.[4]

Doc Searls, author of *The Intention Economy* and a contributor to the groundbreaking *Cluetrain Manifesto*, isn't nearly as diplomatic in his assessment of big data. In a recent *Wall Street Journal* article, Searls wrote:

> ...big business continues to believe that a free market is one in which customers get to choose their captors. Choosing among AT&T, Sprint, T-Mobile and Verizon for your new smartphone is like choosing where you'd like to live under house arrest. It's why marketers still talk about customers as "targets" they can "acquire," "control," "manage" and "lock in," as if they were cattle. And it's why big business thinks that the best way to get personal with customers on the Internet is with "big data," gathered by placing tracking files in people's browsers and smartphone apps without their knowledge—so they can be stalked wherever they go, with their "experiences" on commercial websites "personalized" for them.
>
> It is not yet clear to the perpetrators of this practice that it is actually insane. Think about it. Nobody from a store on Main Street would follow you around with a hand in your pocket and tell you "I'm only doing this so I can give you a better shopping experience."[5]

Central to the problem, as Searls sees it, is that we built our entire twentieth-century marketing paradigm on the premise that supply (not demand) drives the market, and that mass and scale above all else are what drive success and profitability. In a world where supply was scarce, customization was hard and the consumer's ability to find alternatives was limited, retailers could get away with dictating the price and terms of doing business. But in a world where products are commoditized, supply is endless and consumers have the means to discover alternatives, the supplier-dominant model doesn't work anymore. Furthermore, consumers can connect, collaborate and customize with brands more easily and cost effectively than ever before.

Besides, as he correctly points out, for every new tool that marketers acquire to secretly gather and analyze consumer data, consumers find new tools to dodge marketers. Ad blocking, TV-commercial skipping, do-not-track legislation and more defensive measures are all thwarting marketers' attempts to intrude on them. Plugins like Mozilla's *Collusion* can create an instantaneous map of all third parties that are tracking your movements across the web. You can then consciously stop visiting sites that are intrusive. In other words, the better brands become at being predators, the better consumers become at keeping from becoming prey. At this rate, marketers are playing for a draw.

For me though, there's another radically important and completely tangential implication to big data. Something that will simply wipe out any retailer in its path that doesn't see it coming. You see, companies aren't the only ones who will leverage big data for benefit. Consumers too will rapidly begin to tap this entirely new and exponential level of computing and analytical power to guide their attention and buying decisions in a more effective and seamless way than ever before. They'll use the power of big data and other emerging technologies to cut through the sea of products and services available in the market and zero in on the one's that suit them best.

What it constitutes is the emergence of a new destination in retail—soon to be *the preeminent destination.* And one that will make the disruption e-commerce caused seem like a picnic.

The new retail destination I'm referring to is YOU.

SERENDIPITOUS SHOPPING

"Data is not information, and information is not knowledge, and knowledge is not wisdom."

— *Source Unknown*

Based on clues we can see all around us, it is my belief that retail, *as we've known it* for at least the last two millennia, is coming to an end. It won't end tomorrow or next week. In fact, it will likely take at least a decade or two. But it's very clear to me that we are coming to a tipping point and data, processing power and connectedness lie at the center of it all. The reason is this...

Retail has fundamentally always been about destinations. The word *retail* itself is from the French *retaillier*, meaning to divide up and sell in small amounts across multiple locations. As consumers we have always been required to go somewhere to get things we need. Whether it was a market, store, mall, big-box or even the Internet, manufacturers and retailers controlled distribution. We as consumers had to make conscious trips to these destinations and do business on whatever terms were dictated.

And what's interesting is that many of the groups I speak to are dying to know which of these destinations and formats are vanishing, which types of retailing are finished forever.

Ironically, we're not witnessing the absolute death of any particular retail destination, but rather the emergence of a completely new one—You! And not *just* you, but me, too. Every one of us is an individual destination for brands and retailers. Here's where we're headed...

You're on your way to a meeting in Chicago when your mobile device alerts you to the fact that your anniversary (which you forgot) is the day you return home from your meeting. "Damn," you say, startling the cab driver. But not to worry, your digital assistant on your device offers up a list of gift suggestions that you could buy your spouse, knowing his or her preferences, your spending habits, what you've bought your spouse in the past and what your friends are talking about on social networks. She serves these options up for you in a fraction of a second.

Relieved, you choose one of the recommended gifts. She now scours the universe of potential online and offline options based on best price, in-stock availability, fastest shipping, nearest in proximity to your current location and the hotel you're staying at and available loyalty points for redemption as well as any coupons that can be applied. She uses all this data to almost instantly produce a tidy and simple hierarchy of choices and all this in real time. She doesn't need to ask about color choice because she already knows that from past gift purchases for your spouse.

Feeling great about having this gift looked after for you, you select one of the options. Your assistant now processes the transaction on your behalf, disclosing only the amount of information you have pre-authorized, while double-checking to ensure that no tracking or privacy violations have been encountered along the way. She returns with a confirmation that all is in order and wishes you a pleasant trip. And while you're moving and shaking in Chicago, your digital assistant will be tracking the order's progress. Life is good!

What I've just described will, by the year 2022, become a common method of buying a significant percentage of the things we need on a day-to-day basis. The days of consciously having to seek things out, evaluating alternatives with whatever information is available and making purchases based solely on the retailers terms are going to come to an end. Burying tracking cookies in shoppers' browsers or in their devices will seem like something out of the Dark Ages.

The future will see consumers move between *anywhere* convenience and *only-here* experiences.

Increasingly it will not be the consumer who travels to the store, but the products that travel to the consumer in a completely seamless, serendipitous and relevant way. Consumers will regulate their interests, control their privacy and dictate many of the terms of engagement. And if a brand doesn't like it, consumers will simply move down the list until they find one that does.

And where will all this stuff we're buying on the fly be delivered? Well, players like Amazon and 7-Eleven are already testing drop boxes in select 7-Eleven locations, allowing for seven-day-a-week deliveries that consumers can pick up at their convenience. Similarly, Google recently acquired Canadian startup BufferBox, enabling central and convenient 24/7 delivery of online orders. And UK's ShopBox has developed lockable, refrigerated containers that are placed outside the home to hold deliveries of just about anything, including perishables.

This is not a shift from brick and mortar to e-commerce — it's much broader than that. In fact, as we as consumers gradually become the destination, we'll stop discerning so much between online and offline retail. Channels of distribution won't matter. Goods and services will simply come to us or where convenient. Or, when we are given the promise of a memorable, one-of-a-kind live experience, we'll visit a store.

As we move toward this new model, a few important things will be required to fall into place.

1. Re-aggregated Consumer Identities

If marketers were to categorize me as a consumer based solely on my Facebook profile, it certainly wouldn't tell a coherent story. Nor would my activity on eBay be entirely representative of who I am as a consumer. This is why most of the marketing outreach is irrelevant — because it's built on incomplete data. But if you took the sum total of my online and offline shopping and purchase activities on an ongoing basis, paired it with my daily calendar and travel patterns and then added in my banking information and my loyalty programs, a very clearly articulated picture of Doug Stephens, consumer, would soon emerge. It would be possible not only to understand my purchase behavior, but to predict it based on triangulating other data, such as my location, social graph and calendar items. This requires a wholesale reclamation of our often-disparate activities across the web. It requires a wiping of the slate and a fresh start—one profile that explains who we are as consumers.

Author, journalist and entrepreneur John Battelle, who has long been an advocate of what he calls metaservices or "über-applications," which allow us to re-aggregate and manage our social identity across the Internet, believes we are on the cusp of this sort of innovation. Battelle writes,

> For that to happen, every app, every site, and every service needs to be more than just an application or a content directory. It needs to be a platform, capable of negotiating ongoing relationships with other platforms on behalf of its customers in real time. This, of course, is what Facebook does already. Soon, I believe, every single service of scale will work in a similar fashion.
>
> …I think it's only a matter of time—and not much of it—before we have a "metaservice" hit on our hands—an entirely new and delightful service that curates our digital lives and adds value above the level of a single site.[6]

A metaservice that allows us to construct one clear consumer identity is the first essential ingredient for the new era.

2. User Curated Preferences

Because marketers have traditionally crept around quietly, picking up the breadcrumbs of our shopping behaviors, we're often served advertising and recommendations that seem out of whack with our needs and preferences. The new era will give consumers the power to manage their own profiles, declaring their own individual brand, product and service preferences and granting brands permission to access those profiles to serve them.

Tastes, preferences and needs change, and it's essential that we have the ability to manage and evolve these things over time. This will be done using the kinds of recommendation and rating engines we see today on sites like Pandora, Amazon and Netflix. As our digital assistants serve up recommendations for products and services, our satisfaction levels with them will become learned and incorporated into future recommendations. As we add data by "liking" brands on Facebook, "pinning" items on Pinterest or buying things on eBay, our digital assistants will incorporate this knowledge into future recommendations.

As new interests enter and exit our lives, we (and only we) will dial up or down our assistant's awareness and sensitivity to products, services and events that are near us that we may be interested in. For example, eight years ago I became intensely interested in fly-fishing. I damn near OD'd on fly-fishing. In cases like this, I could simply dial up my assistant's sensitivity to all things fly-fishing. When (and if) my obsession subsided, I could simply dial it back down.

As our dependence on digital assistants as our trusted Sherpa guides increases, our awareness and responsiveness to advertising will almost certainly cliff jump, causing no end of trouble for media and advertisers. If a product or service doesn't come to our attention through our assistant, or a close friend, it may as well be invisible. These digital assistants will in essence become our gatekeepers, protecting us from irrelevant and intrusive marketing distractions.

3. Controlled Consumption

In 2003, Oren Etzioni found himself on a plane. The University of Washington professor was traveling to a wedding and, through the course of conversation with other passengers, found that despite booking his ticket well in advance of many of his fellow passengers, he'd paid considerably more for it! Etzioni didn't get mad, however—he got even. The incident prompted him to develop Farecast, a search algorithm that seeks out the best airline fare from point A to B and tells users precisely when to buy their ticket to get the absolute lowest possible fare. In an independent audit, the program proved 70 to 75 percent accurate and was subsequently bought up in 2007 by Bing Travel. Seeing that he was onto something, in 2010, Etzioni expanded his pursuit by creating Decide.com, a recommendation engine that applies the same predictive pricing analysis to thousands of consumer items.[7] Users can quickly determine if now is the best time to buy the thing they need or if they should wait for the price to drop based on heaps of data

Decide.com also takes ancillary considerations like rumors into account. For example, Etzioni points to the number of people who bought items like iPad 1, without being aware of rumors that iPad 2 was weeks away from being announced. His recommendation engine flags this kind of soft data for its users. Furthermore, Decide.com purports to have upwards of 80 percent accuracy in its predictive pricing analytics and backs it with a guarantee that if in fact it drops after a buy-it-now recommendation, Decide will refund buyers the difference in price.

This is precisely this sort of mental gymnastics and legwork that we will look to our digital assistants to perform on our behalf. To pick through the data we have no patience or time for and in a matter of seconds, bring us the results—the prioritized list of the things that most perfectly meet our needs. And nothing else!

In time, there will be very few consumer decisions in our lives that our digital assistants won't be able to help us navigate, and this navigation will not always lead us to a retail transaction in the classical sense.

Now, more than 100 years after retail innovator John Wanamaker began using the first price tags in retail, it will increasingly be we, the consumer who will begin setting the price *we're* willing to pay and waiting for the market to comply.

And doing so, will be requesting that our digital assistant alert us when it finds the product we need at a price that's within our acceptable range. This new era of consumerism will also bring with it entirely new retail buying models, giving consumers new and unprecedented means of getting the things they need with unheard of control.

Scan this for a quick video clip on what I call *serendipitous shopping*.

THE WIN-ME ECONOMY   In the case of major purchases, I agree completely with Doc Searls's assessment that we'll see consumers, where it makes sense, tendering out major purchases like appliances, cars and vacations to the lowest vendor-bidder. We will leverage the network to communicate what we want and the terms we're prepared to buy under, and we'll respond to vendors who are prepared to meet or exceed those terms. We can already see the beginning of this with companies like NetPlenish, who will shop the entire list of everyday food and household items one might need across a group of vendors to determine the lowest total basket price, which it will then send back to you for approval and shipping authorization. In the win-me economy, retailers will not set the terms and prices for their products, but will be required instead to compete for customers by meeting their expressed and specific terms.

THE *TUÁNGÒU* ECONOMY   Originated in China, a *Tuángòu* or organized mob of consumers connects via the Internet and descends en masse on an agreed-upon retail location to demand discounts from the proprietor in return for the entire group buying the same or similar items. In many cases, the merchant has little choice but to capitulate with some form of discount or face the scorn of the mob.

We've come a long way since the first *Tuángòu*, of course, with buying sites like Groupon and others stepping in to do the organizing and negotiating for us. That said, given the ease with which people with common needs or interests can now find and connect with one another across markets, it's inevitable that consumers will increasingly find ways to self-organize into buying groups to offer preferred pricing wherever possible. I mean, if a network can bring down political dictators, surely to God we can leverage our connectedness to buy a few dishwashers or hatchbacks, right? These organically occurring *Tuángòu*s are bound to become an increasingly common phenomenon. Simply, consumers will organize to take collective buying power directly to manufacturers. And they will win.

THE MAKE-IT-YOURSELF ECONOMY Imagine a world where we can quite effortlessly produce many of the household items we need on a daily basis, such as tools, household accessories, toys, etc. What if many of these things could be manufactured in the comfort of our own homes? Picture having the ability to create the things we need, as we need them, one at a time, in any design we prefer.

Now, what if I told you that not only is what I just described possible, but it could also be commonplace by 2020?

3-D printers create objects by stacking layers of material — often metal or plastics — onto one another in the form of the desired object. Designs are based on three-dimensional digital models that can be created using simple and readily available software.

Originally used by manufacturers to build expensive prototypes, the technology is quickly scaling down in affordability with a quality desktop unit for as little as $1,200. And while that might still sound like a pretty steep price tag, consider that the first Sony Betamax retailed for well over $1,000 in 1975 dollars — an astronomical price by today's standards.

It's not difficult to imagine an end state where rather than buying certain household products or decor items, consumers simply purchase the design for a fraction of the price and make the item themselves in a matter of minutes using their 3-D printer.

Technology will increasingly allow us to design and print on demand, more and more of the physical products we need in what ever quantities we want.

4. Calculated and Connected Consumerism

As we fundamentally change the way we buy things, the terms and methods of payment will also have to change. Our digital assistants will run the math for us, taking into consideration things like personal budgeting, available cash or credit on hand and loyalty rewards that can be redeemed. In some cases, we may be initially warned off making a purchase either because the price is higher than average or simply because we don't have the available funds to do so comfortably. Where it makes sense mathematically, our assistant may recommend taking advantage of retailer offers like financing, reward point usage or layaway plans.

Of course, much is being made right now of mobile payment, and while there's little doubt that our archaic forms of currency will disappear sooner or later, there are also some barriers to rapid adoption. The first is the simple fact that our current methods of payment (credit cards, debit cards and cash) aren't broken. They work, we're comfortable with them and there's no inherent friction in using them. Nonetheless, most groups that are promoting the *mobile wallet* are focusing almost purely on mobile payment—something that, at best, is only one small aspect of the value that a truly mobile wallet promises.

Furthermore, our devices themselves aren't entirely reliable or secure. Who wants to be sitting in a restaurant with an important client or a hot date when the bill comes, only to discover the black screen of death on their iPhone, whose battery conked out an hour ago? In order for the true mobile wallet to gain a foothold, we need to be able to depend on the device. This means either longer battery life, significantly lower power usage, more cloud-based processing or the advent of ambient charging almost anywhere payment is required.

So for the mobile wallet to gain meaningful traction a few important things have to happen. Chiefly, our thinking has to move far beyond simple payments and transactions and begin to provide the added value of guiding me to the best shopping outcomes based on my unique tastes and preferences. It has to be far more than just a digital credit card, and instead become the tether that connects all the applications that make me a better and infinitely more intelligent shopper. And do it all reliably, securely and without me having to sweat running out of battery power. When our mobile device truly becomes our digital shopping assistant, then and only then will we leave our cards and cash at home...gladly!

My guess is that it's going to take at least a few years for us to get beyond the fascination phase with mobile payment before we move into some of the richer applications of a true mobile wallet that I've described above. And from there, perhaps another few years before we begin seeing the rise of a true digital shopping assistant.

PICK YOUR METASERVICE   This leads us to the obvious question of which company among us is capable of becoming the kind of consumer metaservice that I've described. A company that knows me; my shopping habits; my schedule, movements and social graph; and my budgetary constraints. A company that I willingly subscribe to in order to manage my consumer life. The answer today, of course, is none. At least no *one* company has all that insight into us as consumers. However, if you look closely, you can see how the big players in the market (especially Google) are each beginning to assemble what look like the components of a metaservice. The ducks are clearly being put in a row. Each of these companies has clearly articulated ambitions to serve as the central marketplace in our lives and they're assembling the artillery to do just that.

Accumulation of metaservice components among major U.S. online players

Facebook	Google	eBay	Amazon	Apple
social	search	shopping	shopping	iOs
photos	video	payment	daily deals	devices
location-based services	location-based services	artificial intelligence	artificial intelligence	payment
shopping	payment	daily deals	payment	shopping
device (rumored)	Android OS	second screen experiences	Kindle device	location-based services
media/ marketing	augmented reality		media/ publishing	voice recognition interface
	artificial intelligence	daily deals	daily deals	
	social			
	voice recognition			
	publishing			

For the record, one could add Walmart and just about every major bank to this race as well.

But who (if any of these) ultimately prevails in this new arms race will depend on a couple of things. First, which of these companies can stitch together all the required applications to dependably and securely guide our consumer lives, and do so through an intuitive and simple user interface? Which has the power to guide us, learning more about us with every query, comment and transaction, helping us to make the best decision in every circumstance and relieving us of much of the drudgery of search and evaluation. And who can do this so well that we become willing, paying subscribers to their service!

The answer lies in which of these we believe in our hearts we can *trust*. To whom can we hand over the open book of our consumer lives and feel confident that they will put our best interests first, protect our personal information and act wisely on our behalf? Which provider can we rely on to show us the best product and service solutions for our needs—not simply what they've negotiated the best affiliate margins on? Who will guard our data like a pit-bull and resist the urge to sell us off to the highest bidder.

This brings me all the way back to the big deal about big data—it's a double-edged sword.

Sure, it has tremendous potential to make retailers better at what they do and contribute to better shopping experiences for consumers. The temptation for many marketers, however, will be to treat big data as a surrogate for mass marketing—something to use to badger and trick consumers more effectively. This is a mistake. Big data can't be looked at as merely another new consumer mousetrap or to simply eke out an extra percentage in profit or dollar in sales. It's not to say that such results can't be byproducts of big data efforts but they ought not to be the sole objective.

Instead, companies need to begin with the philosophical assumption that their big data capabilities can and should actually be used openly to improve the customer's experience and enhance their level of trust in the brand. That the mutual sharing of information can actually lead to *transformational* experiences that solidify the customer's loyalty and passion for the brand and not simply an extra transaction or two. It's a matter of adopting the point of view that the precious insights a company can now mine from its data are not a stolen treasure to be hoarded but rather a gift to be shared graciously with customers. Just as Washington Hospital Center used its big data to ensure the improved health of its patients, retailers must use theirs for the improved happiness of their customers.

This is not an easy transition for retailers. Hell, in the blink of an eye, we're moving from 100 years of mass marketing to a new era of materiality and meaning. We've gone from a place where size and scale trumped all else to a new age where significance and sincerity conquer. From targeting markets to connecting to and conversing with individual customers. From taking to giving. From marketing to executing.

THE END OF MARKETING AS WE KNOW IT

It all prompts what is perhaps the most daunting question of all for retailers. That being, how their businesses would fare in a world where the influence of their marketing pitches is steadily marginalized, if not eliminated.

What if all that marketing window-dressing got stripped away? What if the only considerations between one brand and another were facts and hard metrics about product and service performance, price and genuine reputation? In other words, what if all the marketing bullshit was removed from the equation and every business was essentially evaluated based on how good they really were? If all of a sudden the difference between two hamburger joints became solely about how good their burgers actually are relative to their price and how many positive/negative experiences they've created for customers in their stores as evidenced by honest and measurable ratings—not how funny their TV commercial is or how memorable their radio jingle has become but purely based on an amalgam of factors that equate to a hard-ranking of overall performance. In other words, what if we returned to a world where businesses succeeded because they were excellent, not because they could buy more advertising than anyone else or secure a more creative agency. And what if these supremely rational supplier evaluations were being brought to consumers in a serendipitous way as they went through their day—not for further analysis but merely for a go-ahead to buy.

The signs of such a future are beginning to show themselves. Projects like Google Now give us a glimpse of a future where apps begin to talk and share with one another on a common communication platform to bring us just-in-time information based on where we are and what we're doing in a fluid and predictive way. Facebook Gifts, which not only reminds us of friends birthdays but also recommends gifts based on their LIKES, shows a slice of what's to come when we truly begin to integrate our respective social graphs into our consumer lives to inform purchase decisions. Other startups like Kimera Systems out of Portland, Oregon, are working on taking smartphone intelligence to the next level, to a point where our device begins to not only understand what we need but what we *will* need moments from now — connecting the dots between our calendar, location, shopping, social networks and more. Their goal is to overlay a complete layer of predictive artificial intelligence over every web interaction we have.[8] In short, our digital assistants will not only help us find the things we know we need, when we need them but also predict and present what we're going to need before we know it.

Scan this to watch a video showing Google Now.

And here's the scary bit for marketers...these algorithmic, Hadoop-sifting assistants will be largely unmoved by marketing spin, smoke-and-mirrors pricing games or superfluous retailer claims. They won't care how many ad words you've bought or how much you spent to optimize your website. They will stick unemotionally to what is factual, measurable and real and will promote *only* those brands, offers and retailers that best meet the needs of their users based on fact not fallacious reviews or fictitious brand claims. They will do the math that their owners don't have time to do.

With all this in mind, it leads me to believe that the reign of marketing is coming to a close. But I think we all already feel that in the pit of our stomachs. And the thing keeping more than a few CEO's up at night is that success in business is going to be increasingly about *real performance*—doing what you say you do and doing it excellently well; standing out so distinctly from competitors on every level that you become the default choice—the mathematical certainty.

I'm not suggesting that all shopping decisions will be taken out of the consumer's hands and marketing will completely disappear, but I will argue that these sorts of technologies will easily assist with the majority of routine and unpleasant decisions we have to make each day with less regard for marketing in general. Decisions like where to eat lunch, which cab company to call for a pickup, which airline to book with for my next trip will be all made systematically and unemotionally by our digital assistants. This will free us from mundane consumer legwork and will arguably give us more time to invest in shopping for the things we really are passionate about—the stuff we *want* to be personally involved with.

In preparing for this future, a few questions all businesses should be asking—regardless of what they—sell are…could we survive in a world with a hell of a lot less marketing? Does our business have the chops to withstand the scrutiny of a cloud-based algorithm that can sum up our true performance in an instant? Are we still reliant on buying attention or does our outstanding performance earn it every day?

In other words, how good are we…really?

10

Break It, Build It and Make It Beautiful

BREAK IT

The Barking Frog is a popular bar in the town where my daughter goes to university. As it happens, the bar is located on a street with a number of homes close by. A couple of years ago the bar began to receive complaints from residents about noise levels on the nights when the club would host dance parties, which usually included multiple DJs. To make matters worse, during the summer months the bar features an expansive outdoor patio at the front and side of the building, so partying patrons often spill outside to drink and dance. It made for some pretty noisy nights and a pretty upset neighborhood. In the face of escalating complaints, the bar had to do something.

I love this story because in a very simple way it sums up the dilemma that businesses often find themselves in—confronted with a problem for which there seems to be precious few simple solutions. I'm willing to bet that in this same situation, most bar owners would elect for the safest and most obvious choice: simply turn the music down just enough to make residents less irate, but not so low as to lose too many patrons. Another percentage of owners would go into denial, do nothing and hope the whole thing blows over.

What makes this situation intriguing to me is that the tendency toward incremental change—in this case to turn the music down a little—is a strategic choice we see so many businesses making today. A retailer is getting his lunch eaten by online competitors so he improves his e-commerce capability—a little. A department store finds itself getting killed on price, so it chooses to match competitor prices on select items—but only when customers ask them to. And so it goes, on and on. Little changes that carry low risk. At least, that's what businesses would like to think.

But if we're honest about it, history shows that incremental change rarely does much but forestall the inevitable. Incremental change demands that everyone—employees, customers and suppliers—compromise or change, just a little bit, to deal with an inconvenience. Like an umbrella in a monsoon, it doesn't make a damn bit of difference.

When change is incremental, everyone generally loses—incrementally.

By the same token, burying your head in the sand and hoping the disruption is temporary is usually just as disastrous. Just ask Blockbuster video, Borders bookstores or Avon. Internet video sales were Blockbuster's to lose, but Blockbuster simply did nothing. Borders, like so many other bookstores, could have redefined the book-reading experience—digital or otherwise—but opted instead to outsource digital sales to Amazon and never made the transition in its brick-and-mortar stores. Avon could have used the Internet and social networks to completely redefine the direct sales industry, but it chose to keep pushing the same business model it has had in place for over 100 years.

And this is precisely why I love how the owners of The Barking Frog chose to address the noise issue. Ignoring all the more obvious and safe choices, it instead did something that put the business at risk—something that required a creative leap of faith. The owners turned the bar into a "silent disco." On dance party nights, every patron entering the bar is given a pair of wireless headphones that they wear while they dance. Anyone who wants a conversation can simply take their headphones off. To those entering the bar, the sight of hundreds of gyrating bodies on the dance floor, all of whom are moving somewhat in unison to an inaudible beat, is amazing. The owners quite aptly called these events "Quiet Riots."

Hardly what you would call an incremental change! And unlike stories of innovation from companies like Starbucks or Apple, The Barking Frog is not about a huge company with deep consulting resources. It's not a case of one incredibly visionary leader—a Jobs or a Bezos—making the difference. This was an average business, the kind you'd find anywhere, that made a creatively radical, risky and innovative choice.

The bad news for The Barking Frog—well, actually, there isn't any bad news. In fact, these silent disco nights turned out to be such a huge success that the bar has been holding them ever since. Patrons, most of whom are university students, love the idea. Not only do they get the same great music, but now it doesn't matter how loud it is. People who wouldn't normally frequent this bar (or maybe any bar) came out of interest, and neighborhood residents are sleeping like babies.

When radical innovation is successful, everybody wins exponentially.

If you've taken anything from this book, I hope it's that we are coming to the end of a very long and stable era in consumerism and entering a new one fraught with change. Every day retailers are encountering entirely new challenges and opportunities: new consumer mindsets, new channels, new technologies, new competitors and entirely new approaches to market. The whole notion of what retail is and how it serves consumers or how consumers serve themselves is morphing. It's no longer feasible to simply soldier on, taking action only when the company encounters trouble. Because things are moving so fast, by the time you get the first whiff of trouble, it may already be too late.

It's also time to accept that continuous improvement means nothing when technology is moving so quickly and cheaply that some 18-year-old can potentially invent an app in his parents' basement that kills your business overnight! Incremental change simply will not guard you against these new and profound forms of disruption.

In fact, if there's any way to avoid being victimized by disruption in your category, business or industry, it's by being the one causing it. You (not someone else) need to be the one creating entirely new terms of reference for your industry—rewriting the rules. This will require that the best companies pursue a new strategic objective: to *put themselves out of business.*

You read that correctly. The best companies will constantly find a way to undermine their own business or industry model before someone else does. They will be the first to plan and execute their own overthrow, they will be the masterminds of their own undoing!

If this sounds insane, consider that with the launch of the iPad, Apple essentially lit a short fuse on the MacBook's demise. Similarly, by moving to digital streaming of movies in 2007 (a relatively new model at the time), Netflix put its mail subscription business, which had well over 10 million subscribers at that point, in jeopardy. Both companies created completely new terms of reference in their categories that, even today, their competitors struggle to meet.

The speed and veracity of change simply demands that organizations undertake these sorts of bold and often risky innovations. They need to create new models, methods and measures in their industry that render the status quo irrelevant! They need to find the things that everyone else is missing to create the new industry paradigm. All this means that if your company isn't already masterful at innovating, you need to become so, fast! And if you're not a highly innovative company, don't despair—frankly, most aren't. But it doesn't mean they can't be.

But know this…as long as you're guarding, nurturing and defending the status quo, there will be no innovation of any consequence in your organization.

If you've already made the decision to defy industry paradigms, rebel against tradition and disrupt your own business model, then here are a few humble tips.

BUILD IT

In my experience working with a variety of companies, large and small, particularly on creative teams, I've seen the same cardinal sins committed repeatedly. So, forget about trying to be the next Steve Jobs or Richard Branson. Just *don't* do the following things and I'm pretty certain your organizational innovation quotient will skyrocket.

Don't Innovate with the Wrong People

All too often, when companies are seeking innovation, they recruit precisely the wrong people into the effort.

First and foremost, leaders frequently involve themselves, which can be a fatal mistake. The Wharton School recently released a surprising study that suggested the most creative people in companies are rarely those who are regarded as leaders. It stands to reason, then, that if your CEO, president or VP is a strong leader, then he or she might not be the most wildly creative person in the company. Leadership and creativity, it seems, may be opposing competencies. The problem is this: leaders' ideas regularly get the biggest spotlight and the most support. In other words, with leaders involved, the company runs the risk of giving the worst ideas the most credence.

Then there are the loudmouths—those whose capacity to be heard far outweighs their ability to innovate. Unfortunately, they end up pushing more of their ideas and advocacies through, simply because they were the loudest voice in the conference room. Susan Cain, author of *Quiet: The Power of Introverts in a World That Can't Stop Talking*, says that despite research clearly showing that introverts are often the most creative people in the organization, companies tend to overlook their involvement in creative projects, electing instead to include the most gregarious and outspoken.

Finally, every organization has its guardians of the status quo. These are people who defend *business as usual* like their lives depend on it—because usually their lives do depend on things remaining the same. The touchy thing is that these are also quite often the people who have been with the company the longest, so project leaders feel obliged and even pressured somehow to include them. Unfortunately, in my experience these people have little to offer in the way of radical new thinking, and are usually an impediment to innovation. In fact, many are actually threatened by the very innovation you're asking them to participate in.

When building innovation teams, look for people who are either new to the organization or who bring a variety of experiences with other companies, professions or industries. And don't shut them down when they offer ideas that seem incongruent with company thinking. Presumably, that's why they were hired in the first place! Also, whenever possible, bring in outside and impartial voices to contribute and balance the dialogue. Find sister companies in completely different industries or categories and share people with them who can sit on innovation teams. Fresh thinking is essential, and the more the better.

Don't Make Innovation an Event

There's a great scene in the movie *The Right Stuff*. NASA ground control receives word that there's a problem with the oxygen supply to Apollo 13's service module. With only hours of oxygen left to keep the astronauts alive, experts on the ground spring into action, furiously pouring through possible, innovative solutions to return oxygen supply the to the spacecraft. Within mere hours and just in the nick of time, they innovate a totally unique and never-before-attempted solution, saving all on board and bringing the crew home safely.

There's an important lesson in this scene, and that is that most companies are *not* NASA. Most don't innovate well under extreme pressure. Yet a remarkable number that I have seen and worked with tend only to get passionate about innovation when their backs are against the wall. The truth is that innovation can't be treated as an event or something that's reserved for executive retreats. It has to be a regular, daily organizational pursuit. Google, for example, encourages its staff to spend 20 percent of their time working on any sort of project they want—anything! And aside from the personal satisfaction of doing so, the hope, of course, is that some of these projects may turn into major breakthroughs that return value to the organization. At Google, innovation is a cultural imperative. If you treat innovation as something you do only when you smell smoke, or as an activity between lunch and cocktails, you will suck at it forever.

Don't Talk About Innovation but Reward Compliance

I can't think of a single company that doesn't claim to thrive on innovative thinking. Yet when you delve into most compensation, incentive and performance-management systems, you find that they're incentivizing just the opposite pursuits. Compliance, completion and complicity are what most companies are actually promoting with everything they do. Following the rules, finishing what you start and group thinking are often the most highly rewarded performance dimensions.

"Throughout history, people with new ideas—who think differently and try to change things—have always been called troublemakers."
                        — *Richelle Mead, Author of* Shadow Kiss

---

But innovators often don't fit this mold, and that really shouldn't come as a shock to anyone. By definition, innovation means departing from the norm, breaking the rules and championing often very unpopular thinking. Innovators may be those least likely to play nicely in the sandbox with others or conform to organizational paradigms. They've got their own ideas about things. To be honest, they can often piss people off—not because they're bad people but because they push, challenge and disrupt.

It's worth sitting down with your HR team to ask how many of the company's incentive programs support innovation. If you want innovation, build everything in the organization around promoting, nurturing and rewarding it. Don't fill your innovation teams with a bunch of rule-following yes-men/women. Seek out rebels in the company and make them the example.

Don't Start with the "What" Instead of the "Why"

In an earlier chapter, I shared the vital importance of clearly identifying *why* you do what you do, and stated that this core belief is critical to having a powerful brand. Yet when most companies innovate, they begin by brainstorming ideas about *what* they can do and *how* they can do it, which leads to a very typical list of potential new products and services, improvements to existing products and services, etc., etc. Rarely do companies bother going all the way back to examine why they're in business in the first place, or how the world benefits from their existence. Is the core belief that has been at the center of the company since it started still valid, or is there some other why that may be more current and galvanizing? Let's put it this way: there's a very good chance the world would carry on just fine without whatever product or service you sell, so you need to find another reason…another why… you're in business in the first place.

Try beginning your next innovation session with the question "Why do we exist?" See what happens. (And let me know!)

Don't Focus Creative Energy Inward

Too often innovation work begins by focusing on the company and its problems: the need to raise sales, bolster profit or some other inwardly focused issue. Rarely do companies approach innovation purely from the consumer's point of view, coming up with fresh ideas that will make the life of the customer better, easier or more pleasant. A former colleague of mine used to pull an empty chair up to the table in critical meetings and announce that the consumer was sitting in on the meeting. It just made everyone a little more conscious of the fact that at the end of the day the ideas we generate have to either directly or indirectly benefit our customers. If you don't solve your customers' problems, your problems simply won't matter. In fact, as difficult as it may be, the tougher business becomes and the greater the temptation to be introspective, the more the company needs to focus its energy outward.

It's also critical to resist the temptation to temper every idea against current corporate constraints and limitations. If you frame innovation only within the boundaries of what is feasible through current organizational capacity or ancient organizational history, you will only ever end up very close to where you are right now.

Create the vision first and let another problem-solving team sort out the resource requirements.

Don't Open a New Chapter without Closing This One

Any time a company is preparing to innovate in a major way, it will likely be an unsettling departure from the past—from the way things have been. Yet, these transitions are often so poorly acknowledged by leadership. Companies frequently neglect to bring closure to the current era before moving the organization forward into the next. This leaves everyone feeling somewhat unsettled. It's essential to bring clean closure to the past by commemorating and paying homage to the hard work and commitment that brought the organization to the present. Only then can leaders lay the past to rest and make it clear that a new chapter in the organization's history is about to begin. We need closure before moving on.

Don't Innovate Vertically

Consumers don't measure your company's value and shopping experience purely in comparison with competitors within your specific category. If you sell mobile phones, consumers won't only be judging you relative to other wireless retailers. What matters is how you stack up compared to the many other shopping experiences they have each day in their lives. So if you indeed sell mobile phones, you're being compared to the grocery store, the car rental agency, the coffee shop and any other retailers your customers do business with. For this reason, it's absolutely essential that companies be constantly scanning the environment to find trends, technologies and service approaches outside their categories—"migrateable" learnings that can transform what you do.

Don't Innovate Linearly

Too often, companies confuse innovation and problem solving. In my experience, this is one of the single most significant problems that companies experience.

The mental processes for creating and problem solving are completely different. Problem solving involves linear or vertical thinking. It's orderly, sequential and logical. Creativity requires lateral or horizontal thinking. Innovation is chaotic, spontaneous and passionate. Nobody sent Pablo Picasso off into a meeting room to solve a problem with his art. But all too often innovation sessions begin with leaders presenting the group with a problem to be solved, kicking everyone into linear-thinking mode only to find themselves disappointed at the lack of inspired ideas coming out of the group. I've also been in meetings with teams that just begin to explore very interesting creative spaces and embark on some rich lateral thinking, only to have the CEO or senior person in the room "refocus" everyone on the problem at hand—dragging everyone back into linear mode.

Leaders need to be very clear about what they're looking for—problem solving or innovation. Once they figure that out, then they need to get the hell out of the way.

Lateral thinking is best fed by inputs and stimuli that are non-contextual. For creative geniuses like the Beatles that stimuli was often LSD. You on the other hand need not got to such chemical extremes. But you will need to adjust your thinking to become more expansive. For example, if the end goal is to make your stores more interesting or enriching for consumers, try having a meeting where you do nothing but discuss the heritage of the company or the history of your category, looking in a very relaxed way for elements that can be brought forward or incorporated into what you do today. Or hold your next innovation session in an art gallery and ask your people to find creative inspirations and ideas in the gallery collection that could be employed somehow in your business. Challenge your employees to develop the craziest, weirdest, most outlandish idea that your company has ever seen!

Problem solving is about narrowing and focusing thinking. Innovation is about broadening and expanding thinking. Half of the art of great innovation is recognizing the difference.

MAKE IT BEAUTIFUL

The final evocation I have to offer you may have more to do with life in general than retail specifically, but it's something I believe applies equally to both. Someone I worked with many years ago said that if you look closely at history, you'll quickly see that the only things that survive the test of time are things of great beauty. The Acropolis, the Sistine Chapel, the Mona Lisa, he said, have endured because they are beautiful and we as human beings *want* them to survive and therefore protect them. Ugly things, he argued, may serve a function for a short period, but they never have the longevity of beauty. Beauty wins in the long run every time.

"A thing of beauty is a joy forever: its loveliness increases; it will never pass into nothingness."

—John Keats

Following this logic has never led me astray. Whether it's a mobile app, a store, a company's mission statement or a website, those that are the most beautiful and elegant tend to outperform alternatives over time. So, whatever you build, please strive to make it beautiful. Aspire to make the world a better and more beautiful place by virtue of what your business brings to it.

"The future will be better tomorrow."

—Dan Quayle

By a stroke of brilliant coincidence, we find ourselves at an amazing junction in history. The fat and lazy era in consumerism is giving way to a lean, creative and inspired age. This is the most exhilarating, fascinating and wonderful time in the history of retail. It's the threshold of a tremendous new and infinitely more meaningful era for remarkable companies and their customers. For the first time in over a century, it's going to be possible for the small remarkable retailer to *earn* their customers on the same order of magnitude that a large (but merely average) retailer can buy them. The playing field is leveling. It is indeed a retail revival and a return to the positive social, economic and human value of shopping. But thriving in it will require enormous courage, curiosity and willingness to imagine entirely new and radical ways of doing business.

Don't be afraid. Be bold in reimagining *your* business! Don't waste time. There's simply none to waste. Above all, enjoy every moment of this incredible, bright new era!

ABOUT THE AUTHOR

THE FOUNDER OF RETAIL PROPHET, Doug Stephens is one of the world's most respected and influential retail industry futurists and advisers. His work and thinking have influenced many of North America's best-known retailers and brands, including Walmart, Home Depot, Razorfish, Disney, Loblaws, WestJet, Citibank and Air Miles to name a few.

Drawing on over 20 years of international experience in the retail industry, including the leadership of one of New York City's most historic retail chains, Stephens tracks key shifts in economics, demographics, technology and media to assemble a complete and credible picture of how retail and consumerism is evolving.

He is a highly sought-after keynote presenter, speaking regularly to diverse business and government audiences across North America and Europe about the key changes in consumer behavior and technology that are central to the success of organizations and entrepreneurs.

He is also a regular contributor on the acclaimed television series App Central TV, a retail business contributor for CBC Radio, and a frequent source of opinion for global business media. Stephens sits on the advisory boards of a mobile technology company and the Dx3 digital conference.

Follow Doug on Twitter @Retail Prophet.

ENDNOTES

CHAPTER 1

1. Dov Seidman, "The Economy: Don't Reach for the Reset Button," *Businessweek*, May 18, 2010, http://www.businessweek.com/managing/content/may2010/ca20100517_722611.htm.
2. Tyson Freeman, "The 1960s: Prosperity Spurs Malls, Hotels in Technicolor Dream," *National Real Estate Investor*, September 30, 1999, http://nreionline.com/mag/real_estate_prosperity_spurs_malls/.
3. Amy Traub and Catherine Ruetschlin, "The Plastic Safety Net: Findings from the 2012 National Survey on Credit Card Debt of Low- and Middle-Income Households," Dēmos, May 22, 2012, http://www.demos.org/sites/default/files/publications/PlasticSafetyNet-Demos.pdf.

CHAPTER 2

1. Elizabeth Warren, "The Middle Class on the Precipice: Rising Financial Risks for American Families," *Harvard Magazine*, January–February 2006, http://harvardmagazine.com/2006/01/the-middle-class-on-the-html.
2. Dow Jones Monthly Chart, 1971–2012, The Privateer.com http://www.the-privateer.com/chart/dow-long.html.

3. Congressional Budget Office report, "Historical Effective Federal Tax Rates: 1979 to 2005," December 11, 2007, http://www.cbo.gov/publication/41654.
4. Timothy Noah, *The Great Divergence: America's Growing Inequality Crisis and What We Can Do about It* (New York: Bloomsbury, 2012).

CHAPTER 3

1. Arthur L. Stinchcombe, "Social Structure and Organizations," in *Handbook of Organizations*, ed. James G. March (New York: Rand McNally, 1965), 154.
2. "Families versus Households." *Retailing 2015: New Frontiers*, PricewaterhouseCoopers and TNS Retail Forward, 2007.
3. D'Vera Cohn et al., "Barely Half of U.S. Adults Are Married—A Record Low," The Pew Research Center, December 14, 2011, http://www.pewsocialtrends.org/2011/12/14/barely-half-of-u-s-adults-are-married-a-record-low/; Garret Keizer, "Homeword Bound: The Rise of Multigenerational and One-Person Households," *New York Times*, March 2, 2012, http://www.nytimes.com/2012/03/04/books/review/the-rise-of-multigenerational-and-one-person-households.html.
4. "America's Children in Brief: Key National Indicators of Well-Being, 2012." Child Stats.Gov: Forum Child and Family Statistics, http://www.childstats.gov/americaschildren/demo.asp.
5. "Four in 10 Children Are Born to Unwed Mothers." Familyfacts.org, http://www.familyfacts.org/charts/205/four-in-10-children-are-born-to-unwed-mothers.
6. "Single Parent Statistics." *Single Parent Magazine,* June 2012, http://www.singleparentmagazine.net/single-parent-statistics/.
7. "Shoppers 'Buy Brands for Pleasure Rush' - Study." Digital Strategy Consulting, May 3, 2012, http://www.digitalstrategyconsulting.com/intelligence/2012/03/shoppers_buy_brands_for_pleasu.php.

8. Mitra Toossi, "Labor Force Change, 1950–2050," *Monthly Labor Review*, U.S. Bureau of Labor Statistics, May 2002.

9. Farhad Manjoo, "The Best Reason Yet to Ditch Gmail," *Slate*, July 31, 2012, www.slate.com/articles/technology/technology/2012/07/outlook_webmail_microsoft_s_new_email_service_looks_great_and_doesn_t_invade_your_privacy_.html.

10. Patrick J. Kiger "Boomers' 'Anxiety Index' High, Voter Survey Reveals: Retirement prospects top economic issues, concerns." August 22, 2012, AARP, http://www.aarp.org/politics-society/government-elections/info-08-2012/aarp-2012-voter-survey.html.

11. "Transition Boomers and Retirement Income Survey." The Allianz Life, June 6–8, 2012.

12. "Debt of the Elderly and Near Elderly 1992–2007." Employee Benefit Research Institute, http://www.ebri.org/publications/notes/index.cfm?fa=notesDisp&content_id=4383.

13. "Population by Race and Age: Data." 2010 *U.S. Census Report,* http://2010.census.gov/2010census/.

14. Tavia Grant and Janet McFarland, "Generation Nixed: Why Canada's Youth Are Losing Hope for the Future," *Globe and Mail*, October 27, 2012.

15. Kit Yarrow and Jayne O'Donnell, *Gen BuY: How Tweens, Teens and Twenty-Somethings Are Revolutionizing Retail* (San Francisco: Jossey-Bass, 2009).

16. U.S. Department of State, Office of the Historian, "Milestones: 1921–1936: The Immigration Act of 1924 (The Johnson-Reed Act)," accessed November 7, 2012, http://history.state.gov/milestones/1921-1936/ImmigrationAct.

17. Jeffrey D. Schultz et al., *Encyclopedia of Minorities in American Politics: Vol. 1, African Americans and Asian Americans* (Phoenix, AZ: Oryx Press, 2000).

18. "The Rise of Asian Americans," The Pew Research Center, June 19, 2012, http://www.pewsocialtrends.org/2012/06/19/the-rise-of-asian-americans.

19. *Multicultural Marketing Seminar*: Canadian Marketing Association. http://www.the-cma.org/education-events/multicultural-marketing-seminar

20. Joel Kotkin, "Declining Birthrates, Expanded Bureaucracy: Is U.S. Going European?" *Forbes*, August 15, 2011, http://www.forbes.com/sites/joelkotkin/2011/09/15/declining-birthrates-expanded-bureaucracy-is-u-s-going-european/.

21. From interview with Seth Godin on CBC Television's *The Hour,* January 3, 2012, http://www.youtube.com/watch?feature=player_embedded&v=JJj_WHCdLtQ#!

CHAPTER 4

1. Photo credits: Tony the Tiger, CP Photo/Don Denton; Mr. Clean: AP Photo/Al Behrman; Kentucky Fried Chicken, AP Photo/Eugene Hoshiko; Maytag, Canadian Press/Boris Supremo.

2. Photo credit: James Watson and Francis Crick, Canadian Press.

3. "TV Costs and CPM Trends-Network TV Daytime," Television Bureau of Advertising, http://www.tvb.org/trends/4718/4706.

4. "Our History," Home Depot corporate website, https://corporate.homedepot.com/OurCompany/History/Pages/default.aspx.

5. Best Buy and *WSJ* reporting, "Looking for a Change at Best Buy," *Wall Street Journal*, 2012, http://online.wsj.com/article/SB10001424052702304299304577350223835262792.html.

6. "Internet Usage Statistics: The Internet Big Picture," Internet World Stats, June 30, 2012, http://www.internetworldstats.com/stats.htm.

7. Erik Sass, "Winners and Losers: The Changing Media Ad Landscape, 1980–2011," *Media Daily News*, September 2, 2011, http://www.mediapost.com/publications/article/157452/winners-and-losers-the-changing-media-ad-landscap.html.

8. "How Many Websites Are Their?" Business Insider, March 8, 2012, http://articles.businessinsider.com/2012-03-08/tech/31135231_1_websites-domain-internet

9. Sucharita Mulpuru et al., "US Online Retail Forecast, 2011 to 2016: eCommerce Tops $200 Billion in 2011," Forrester Research, Inc., February 27, 2012, http://www.forrester.com/US+Online+Retail+Forecast+2011+To+2016/fulltext/-/E-RES60672.

10. "Two Millionth Passenger Vehicle Sold on eBay Motors," eBay Inc., August 8, 2006, http://www.ebayinc.com/content/press_release/20060808206868.

11. "U.S. Consumer Direct Wine Sales Hit Record $3.4 Billion in 2010," *Western Farm Press*, May 26, 2011, http://westernfarmpress.com/grapes/us-consumer-direct-wine-sales-hit-record-34-billion-2010.

12. Lev Grossman, "You—Yes, You—Are TIME's Person of the Year," *Time*, December 25, 2006, http://www.time.com/time/magazine/article/0,9171,1570810,00.html.

CHAPTER 5

1. Trond Riiber Knudsen et al., "The Vanishing Middle Market," *McKinsey Quarterly*, November 2005, http://www.mckinseyquarterly.com/The vanishing middle market 1687.

2. Paul Hunt, "Co-branding with Discount Retailers Could Spell Trouble for Exclusive Brands," *Financial Post*, August 31, 2012, http://business.financialpost.com/2012/08/31/co-branding-with-discount-retailers-could-spell-trouble-for-exclusive-brands/.

3. Rhiannon Batten, "Insiders' Guide to the World's Best Shops," *Guardian*, December 9, 2011, http://www.guardian.co.uk/travel/2011/dec/09/worlds-best-shops-shopping-experts.

4. Simon Sinek, "How Great Leaders Inspire Action," filmed September 2009, TEDx Puget Sound, 8:07, posted May 2010, http://www.ted.com/talks/simon_sinek_how_great_leaders_inspire_action.html.

5. Rory Sutherland, "Sweat the Small Stuff," filmed April 2010, TEDSalon London 2010, posted June 2010, http://www.ted.com/talks/rory_sutherland_sweat_the_small_stuff.html.

CHAPTER 6

1. Mitch Joel, "Consumers Control the Brand (And Other New Media Myths)," *Huffington Post*, February 21, 2012, http://www.huffingtonpost.ca/mitch-joel/consumer-brand-marketing_b_1287789.html.

2. Jay Rayner, "Booths: The Honest Supermarket," *Guardian*, November 13, 2011, http://www.guardian.co.uk/business/2011/nov/13/supermarkets-big-competition-booths.

3. Katie Rogers, "Chick-fil-A CEO Puts an End to Speculation, Comes Out...as Anti-Gay," *Guardian*, July 19, 2012, http://www.guardian.co.uk/world/us-news-blog/2012/jul/19/chick-fil-a-comes-out-as-anti-gay.

4. "Who Is John Galt?" Lululemon community blog, November 2, 2011, http://www.lululemon.com/community/blog/who-is-john-galt/.

5. David Welch, "Wal-Mart Beats Amazon Prices Including 'Glee' DVD Set," Bloomberg, June 22, 2012, http://www.bloomberg.com/news/2012-06-22/wal-mart-beats-amazon-prices-including-glee-dvd-set.html.

6. Kim Peterson, "Why Amazon Is Crushing Best Buy," MSN Money, April 4, 2012, http://money.msn.com/top-stocks/post.aspx?post=363b3891-d5ac-49b9-8da4-402b3bc32d73.

7. Kat Matfield, "Bad Reviews Are Good for Business—Really!" Reveoo, January 10, 2012, http://www.reevoo.com/blog/bad-reviews-are-good-business-really.

8. "Flawsome: Why Brands that Behave More Humanly, Including Showing Their Flaws, Will Be Awesome," Trendwatching.com, April 2012, http://trendwatching.com/trends/flawsome/.

9. Jan Rezab, "Companies Respond to Just 5% of Questions on Facebook," Econsultancy, October 17, 2011, http://econsultancy.com/ca/blog/8149-companies-respond-to-just-5-of-questions-on-facebook.

10. "Genesys Research Finds Big Business Still Uneasy with Customer Service Conversations Over Social Media," Genesys, August 23, 2012, http://www.genesyslab.com/news-and-events/press-releases/genesys-research-finds-big-business-still-uneasy-with-customer-service-conversations-over-social-media.aspx.

11. Patrick Enright, "Even Stars Get Stage Fright," Mental health on NBCNEWS.com, September 12, 2007, http://www.msnbc.msn.com/id/20727420/ns/health-mental_health/t/even-stars-get-stage-fright.

———

CHAPTER 7

1. Christopher Matthews, "Can Robots Bring Manufacturing Jobs Back to the U.S.?" *Time,* September 27, 2012, http://business.time.com/2012/09/27/can-robots-bring-back-manufacturing-jobs-to-the-u-s/.

2. "U.S. Shoppers Value the Choice of Self-Service When Shopping," NCR, October 5, 2011, http://www.ncr.com/newsroom/resources/self-service-survey-us.

3. Matthew Dalton, "Europe's Warm Feelings for Robots," *Wall Street Journal,* September 19, 2012, http://blogs.wsj.com/brussels/2012/09/19/europes-warm-feelings-for-robots/.

4. James Surowiecki, "The More the Merrier," *New Yorker,* March 26, 2012, http://www.newyorker.com/talk/financial/2012/03/26/120326ta_talk_surowiecki#ixzz27ar8M3L3.

5. Robin Lewis and Michael Dart, *The New Rules of Retail: Competing in the World's Toughest Marketplace* (New York: Palgrave Macmillan, 2010).

6. Lauren Indvik, "You Can Now Order Made-to-Measure Suits via iPad App in Nordstrom," Mashable, September 3, 2012, http://mashable.com/2012/03/08/joseph-abboud-custom-suits-ipad-app-nordstrondm/.

7. From interview with Mike Wittenstein, September 2012.

CHAPTER 8

1. Patrick Spenner, "Marketers Have it Wrong: Forget Engagement, Consumers Want Simplicity," *Forbes*, July 2, 2012, http://www.forbes.com/sites/patrickspenner/2012/07/02/marketers-have-it-wrong-forget-engagement-consumers-want-simplicity/.
2. Jon Russell, "Smartphone Ownership Passes 50% in Korea, as Authorities Salute the Productivity Benefits," The Next Web Asia, May 15, 2012, http://thenextweb.com/asia/2012/05/15/smartphone-ownership-passes-50-in-korea-as-authorities-salute-the-productivity-benefits/.
3. "Introduction: The Perspective of Seoul Metro," Seoul Metro official website, https://www.seoulmetro.co.kr/eng/page.jsp?code=A020000000/.
4. Retail Prophet, Interview with Gary Schwartz, September 2012.
5. "In Brazil, Campaign Offers Test Drives to Broken Down Motorists," Springwise.com, July 24, 2012, http://www.springwise.com/automotive/in-brazil-marketing-campaign-offers-test-drives-broken-drivers/.
6. Augmented Reality: The Impending Battle for Digital Real Estate: Retail Prophet September 23, 2010, http://www.retailprophet.com/blog/2010/09/23/augmented-reality-the-impending-battle-for-digital-real-estate/.

CHAPTER 9

1. Farhad Manjoo, "Big Changes Are Ahead for the Health Care Industry, Courtesy of Big Data," *Fast Company*, June 18, 2012, http://www.fastcompany.com/1839285/big-changes-are-ahead-health-care-industry-courtesy-big-data.
2. Josh Catone, "How Much Data Will Humans Create & Store This Year?" Mashable.com, June 28, 2011, http://mashable.com/2011/06/28/data-infographic/.

3. "Telefonica Hopes 'Big Data' Arm Will Revive Fortunes," BBC News.com: Technology, October 9, 2012, http://www.bbc.co.uk/news/technology-19882647.

4. Janna Anderson and Lee Rainie, "The Future of Big Data," PewInternet.org, July 20, 2012, http://pewinternet.org/Reports/2012/Future-of-Big-Data.aspx.

5. Doc Searls, "The Customer as a God," *Wall Street Journal*, July 20, 2012.

6. John Battelle, "File Under: Metaservices, The Rise Of," John Battelle's Searchblog, November 9, 2012, http://battellemedia.com/archives/2011/02/file_under_metaservices_the_rise_of.php.

7. "Oren Etzioni," University of Washington website, http://www.cs.washington.edu/people/faculty/etzioni.

8. Dan Rowinski, "What if Your Smartphone Could Read Your Mind? Kimera Is Working on It," ReadWriteWeb, October 11, 2012, http://www.readwriteweb.com/mobile/2012/10/kimera-creates-artificial-intelligence-for-smartphones.php.

INDEX